Angels
in Alaska

Photos courtesy of Bontrager/Hoover families.

ISBN 979-8-6381-8840-5

Book design by Longworth Creative, LLC

First Edition
Printed in the United States of America

Angels
in Alaska

My Adventure with
Elisabeth Kübler-Ross

Leota Hoover

*A percentage of the proceeds from the sale
of this book will go to Marley House, a sanctuary
for dying patients cared for by Hospice.*

CONTENTS

FOREWORD

Leota gave us her final draft of this memoir shortly before she died from the ravages of breast cancer. We had no idea she'd been known as Jan before we knew her. That secret was revealed as we read the early versions of this memoir.

When we met her, in 1994, she was learning to write personal essays at our local college. She said she needed a small group of writers with whom she could improve her efforts, so she organized a dedicated critique group. We came together, a band of eight, and met at the local library to read and critique each other's writing.

We were mesmerized by Leota's accounts of the life she'd lived before we knew her—a childhood in Appalachia, her marriage to an abuser in Alaska, life as a single mother, her debilitating stroke. Later, her breast cancer inspired amusing and heart-breaking essays. Some were published, bringing her notice as an author.

Leota's most compelling stories were the revelations she gave us—in agonizing truthfulness—about her experiences serving as a counselor under the guidance of Elisabeth Kübler-Ross. That period in Leota's life became this fully-realized memoir. We listened to her read chapters, gave her feedback, and followed her journey until her cancer became overwhelming.

After her death in October 2014, we took the manuscript she had put in our hands and polished it as a group effort—making very few changes and taking care to preserve the funny, tough, self-revealing voice that was Jan/Leota.

Elaine Jordan
Prescott, AZ

The Critique Group
Carole Bolinski
Gretchen Brinck, editor
Elaine Jordan
Carrie Malinowski
Colette Ward
Vicky Young

With early support from:
Ben Bakke
Abby Carpenter
Lee Reeves

Leota and Elizabeth Kübler-Ross at an early workshop
1980s

CHAPTER ONE

The Angel Problem

I DIDN'T WANT to meet people who were dying. What was there to say to someone with terminal cancer? Sick people made me nervous and I avoided them. I was an addictions counselor, not a nurse, and unlike one of my cousins, I'd never wanted to be a nurse. I wasn't the sentimental type who went all dewy-eyed and helpful around unhealthy or impaired people. My cardinal rule—never, never, never make eye contact with the dying.

So why was I on my way to a Life, Death, and Transition (LDT) Workshop where I'd be locked in for five days at a remote lodge with terminally ill cancer patients? Angels, those damn Angels, had gotten me into yet another difficult situation. I thought that when the fundamentalist preacher had stormed into my office and threatened to name me as a witch from his pulpit, it was as bad as things could get. I was wrong.

Last year, Connie, our receptionist at the Matanuska-Sutsina Valley Council on Alcoholism and Drug Abuse (Mat-Su Council for short) had placed a *Playboy* magazine on my desk—opened to an interview with Dr. Elisabeth Kübler-Ross, who was famous for her near-death studies. Her 1969 book *On Death and Dying* had changed how medical people and others treat the dying.

With one blood-red fingernail, Connie underscored spirit guides, out of body travel, mystical experiences. Hand on hip and wearing a know-it-all expression, she said, "I'll bet this woman could fix your Angel problem," and swished out of my office.

I'd only skimmed the paragraphs where the doctor answered questions about her work with dying patients, but when she wrote of conversations with her spirit guides, I became attentive. She wasn't a yogi, a spiritualist, or a channel. She wasn't any of the kind of folks

I labeled kooks or crooks. She was a doctor, a psychiatrist, and she spoke of experiences similar to my Angel visitors.

Maybe Connie was right; maybe Dr. Elisabeth Kübler-Ross could sort out my Angel problem. Hope flared, then died. According to the article, she was world famous and lived in California. What chance did I have to talk with her? I was a single mother of three living thirty-three miles from Anchorage, Alaska, in Wasilla, population 1500. I had no money to travel to California, and a renowned figure of her caliber wasn't likely to visit our small town. I closed the magazine and forgot about Dr. Kübler-Ross and her spirit guides.

Yet here I was, one year later—May, 1981—on my way to attend her Life, Death, and Transition Workshop only seven miles from my Alaska home. Dr. Kübler-Ross would be teaching health-care workers and clergy how to work effectively with terminally ill patients. Not only was I attending, I was doing so for free; the Alcoholism Council was paying for Art, my clinical supervisor, and me to be there.

The Angels were taking credit for bringing all this together. I'd come to know these Angels as bossy, inconvenient, controlling non-beings: a damn nuisance. They disrupted my life and caused me to fear for my sanity and reputation.

Family home in Wasilla, Alaska

I'd wondered if I could be schizophrenic or if perhaps I'd experienced a psychotic break. Or did I suffer from a personality disorder or egomania? After all, the voices did call themselves Angels. Was I a garden-variety nut?

*

On many occasions over the previous two years, I'd cursed that summer evening when I yelled "come in" to my ditzy friend Betty when she knocked on my door. In she waltzed, a bottle of wine in one hand and a Ouija board in the other. She had her frizzy red hair tied back with a bright scarf and wore one of her Hawaiian caftans under a green parka. Her Gypsy looks contrasted with my yellow sweats and blond hair—and blue-eyed naiveté.

We chatted, drank some wine, and got out the Ouija board. I hadn't seen one before, but Betty seemed to know the rules. The two of us sat in my ladder-backed dining chairs, faced each other, our knees almost touching, the Ouija board balanced between us. Betty explained that we needed to close our eyes and imagine we were inside a circle of white light "for protection"—from what, she didn't explain, or maybe the wine shielded me from hearing. We placed our fingers atop the droplet-shaped platform—the planchette, she called it—that rested on three felt-tipped feet and had a circular cutout in the pointed end.

We giggled like ten-year-olds at a slumber party (probably the influence of the wine) and waited for something to happen. After a second glass of wine and a few cigarettes, the pointer moved.

"Are you there?" Betty asked, and the pointer moved until yes was visible through the round window. I thought she could have posed a more interesting question, but this was Betty's show. My role was to lend energy, not commentary. I itched to photograph this moment but didn't want to interrupt, and, anyway, the camera wouldn't capture the pointer's movements.

"Will you tell us the truth?" Betty asked. Again the pointer traveled to yes. "Will you lie to us?" It scooted to the opposite corner and rested over no. Thus my dear friend tested the honesty of what I considered a figment of her imagination. I was amused.

What followed was Betty asking a series of questions about the figment, whose name was Sara. How had she died? When and where had she lived? Had she married? Did she have children? It was like reading a poorly written romance novel. I lost interest until the planchette got frisky and moved off the board and down my leg. It felt creepy and I put it back on the board, only to have it continue to move off the board and back onto my leg. When we could no longer keep it on the board, I suggested we move the planchette to the table top. My shoulders were getting tired, and the thing was no longer traveling on the printed board anyway.

Betty and I and the wine reasoned that if we could move the pointer, we could move other objects. I believe the wine suggested the one-pound cut-glass ashtray half full of Viceroy butts. Betty gave it instructions as if it understood. To signal yes, the ashtray was to move forward and backward between Betty and me. A no answer required movement from left to right. With the authority of a drill sergeant Betty barked, "Show us a yes," and the ashtray moved back and forth and stopped dead center. More giggles. "Show us a no," she continued, and it moved left to right. "Show us a maybe," and it moved in a circle.

My memories of that evening are of warm feelings and fun. I loved spending time with my friend.

The troubling Angels didn't arrive until the following week.

Again Betty and I, no wine this time, were experimenting with moving objects around in response to yes and no questions when I wondered what might happen if we used a pen. I placed a small notepad on the table, held a pen in my right hand, and Betty cupped her hands around mine. Very slowly and jerkily, the pen moved across the paper. My whole body trembled. I felt different than when we moved the ashtray.

Always the one to take the lead in activities of the weird and super-natural, Betty asked, "I wonder what would happen if we took the top off the pen?"

I felt a bit silly but uncapped the pen and held it to the paper. I was ready to give it up as a bad idea when I felt an opposing force press against my knuckles. My hand snuggled into the resistance. The pen moved on the page and made squiggly lines. When the squiggles covered the small piece of paper from edge to edge, the trembling left my body, the pressure left my knuckles and the pen fell from my hand.

"This is the craziest thing I've ever done—sober that is." I gathered up our coffee cups, rinsed them at the sink and put them in the dishwasher.

"Hey, this is a word!" Betty had turned the paper on its side and spelled aloud, "A-l-p-h-a."

"If it's a word, it'll be in the dictionary, right?" I jeered. "And if it's not, I quit. No more. Not another word. Right?" Betty agreed and I fetched the *American Heritage Dictionary* from my desk. Confident that this would put an end to the hocus pocus, I opened the book between us and searched through the A words. Then I felt a jolt, like when a fast elevator jerks to a stop. I'd been betrayed by the highest authority of the land— my beloved dictionary.

Betty read, "al·pha. noun. 1. The first letter of the Greek alphabet. 2. The first one; the beginning." She jumped up out of her chair. "I knew it! I knew it!" She squealed and spun around like a kid, her dark-rooted red hair bouncing on her shoulders.

Since that inauspicious beginning, something—something that I eventually decided to call "the Angels"—had been writing lessons, health advisories, past life analysis, legal advice, warnings of impending danger, dental diagnoses, and the reason why three horses had jumped a fence in Utah. (This last was due to a pre-dawn telephone call from a stranger who got my phone number from a friend of a friend of a friend.)

Angel writings had been my life for the past two years: Angels whispered in my left ear, refused to be ignored and wrote notes to anyone through me. Their words simply traveled through my right hand onto paper from wherever the Angels were—in my brain or an invisible someplace. My own will had no part of it. I finally understood, about six months after their first visit, that I had no choice but to deliver their messages to whomever needed them. Since then, I'd had to pay my bills in cash because whenever I tried to write a check my hand would do nothing but transfer any undelivered Angel message, word for word, and I would then need to get it to the intended person.

At times, I felt special and liked the attention. Mostly, I feared doing harm. What if I passed on an Angel message that wasn't true or caused pain or wrongdoing? So far, in the realm of accuracy and diplomacy, the Angels had scored one hundred percent, but I had no guarantee that would continue. The bits of information I dug up at the tiny local library said that for 100 or more years, spiritualists and others believed that spirits channeled messages through certain people by means of this automatic writing and that it could sometimes happen through using Ouija boards. The information didn't solve the mystery of why me or who these Angels were.

The biggest question was—why me? What right did I have to go mucking around in the lives of others? Angels or no Angels, I knew I wasn't a saint. I wasn't a witch either, although there were rumors that said differently. I was just a generic single mother of three who wanted to do the right thing and get by the best I could. Yet my life turned upside down when the Angels came into my life.

I wanted to talk to someone about the Angels who wouldn't automatically discount me as a loon or regard me as a holy messenger. I reasoned that Dr. Kübler-Ross was an authority, someone who didn't live in la-la-land, and she was known for believing in spirit guides and such; maybe she could explain what had happened to me. When I saw she'd be teaching nearby, I signed on.

But how had I missed that the sick and dying would be present at the workshop called Life, Death, and Transition? I'd scanned the release, but it appeared to have been revised since my signing. When I reread the rules, phrases that I could swear weren't there before, leapt to my attention, like: "terminally ill patients will be in attendance."

I was on my way to spend five days with people who were dying!

CHAPTER TWO
No Way Out

GENTLE JEFF, a Vietnam vet who lived in my laundry room, volunteered to drive me to the Life, Death, Transition workshop. Art, my supervisor, would find his way on his own; we'd meet at the lodge. I sat in the passenger seat of my twelve-year-old Volvo for the seven mile drive north to the Meier Lake Conference Center. It was the first week of May, still in that season Alaskans call "breakup"—the time when frozen rivers and lakes begin to melt and ice chunks violently crash into each other. A time of unrelenting ice and mud that served as Alaska's frigid spring.

Jeff approached the unpaved parking lot of the lodge with care. Cars were parked every which way, and the area had wooden walkways that eliminated the need for boots. The two-story, square, windowless main building was not what I'd expected. Lodges were supposed to be made of logs, but this was a clapboard box painted an uninviting reddish brown. There were small log cabins scattered along the walkways that wound through the spruce forest, but the cabins looked cold, sitting as they did under the trees; no sunlight could possibly warm them and I saw no chimneys or vents. How were they heated?

Oh, great! On top of everything else, I was expected to freeze.

As I exited the car, I reminded Jeff not to vacuum until I got home on Friday. In my absence, he was to care for the kids and Sump'n, my obese black and white Chihuahua. Jeff reassured me he'd be careful not to vacuum, and that he'd look for the ring I'd lost the night before. Ugly as it was, that ring meant a lot to me. Jeff had helped Travis, my ten-year-old son—who was blonde and blue-eyed like me—carve the ring out of moose horn. It had been Travis's birthday present to me.

In a way, Jeff was a gift as well; he'd come for Thanksgiving dinner a couple of years ago and never left. With scrap lumber from construction sites, he'd fashioned a cave of sorts in my laundry room and drifted in and out of our lives, ghost-like. Days passed and we didn't see him, but he was always there with a helping hand when needed. He and Travis had forged a bond and stood together in a household of females.

With my duffle and sleeping bag at my feet, I stood on the wide porch that ran the length of the lodge and watched Jeff drive out of sight. No way out now. I fished in my purse for my old friends, Viceroy 100s. It was only noon and I'd already smoked half a pack. "My roommate could be one of the sick or dying" would pop into my head and I'd light up.

I walked slowly around the porch, then hooked my jean-clad butt over the railing, lit up, and sucked in smoky comfort. When I finished my cigarette, I felt more in control. Gone was my last excuse to delay. I flushed my lungs with cold spring air and pushed open the lodge door.

I stepped into blaring light. The wall opposite the door was glass and looked out onto a glacier-fed lake that reflected snow-covered mountains. A narrow pebbly beach circled the lake and separated it from the black spruce forest. I thought, what a perfect illustration of May in Alaska, cold in midday bright light—each detail in sharp focus. Even as I calculated the exposure settings (f/16 at 200), I knew it would be an uninteresting photo, because the 35mm film wouldn't capture the grandeur. My little camera was at home anyway; I dreamed of the day I'd own a large format camera and become a professional photographer.

I turned away from the view and found myself in an uninteresting room filled with people and long tables that smelled of warm bread and apples. I was assigned a cabin number and told to help myself to the buffet; the workshop room was downstairs and we would start in an hour.

About one hundred strangers sat at communal tables and appeared to be trying too hard, smiling too much, talking too loud, and laughing too often. I took an empty seat and kept my eyes on the beige plastic plate before me. It was my ten-inch circle of safety; I could look at it and it wouldn't talk to me. Best of all, it wasn't sick or dying. I told myself I was on a fool's errand and would have left that minute if Jeff hadn't taken my car.

A sudden quiet drew me out of myself. My companions all looked to the exterior door through which entered a small woman. I'd seen bigger ten-year-olds. She was haggard and crumpled, mauled actually. Not only were her drawstring trousers and sweatshirt wrinkled, the person herself seemed wrinkled. Her thin hair could have been styled by a kindergartener and not combed after a fitful night's sleep.

Dr. Elisabeth Kübler-Ross was a mess.

She crossed the long narrow dining room and sat in the recently vacated chair across from me. She leaned forward, and in throaty, accented words asked, "Do you live near here?" I nodded yes, unable to speak around a mouthful of food. "You have a car?" I chewed fast in an attempt to empty my mouth and nodded yes again. "Goot. You take me for tour on Wednesday." She then stood and left the room before I could utter a word.

Would the gentle veteran, my Jeff, be able to deliver the car to me that day? Lunch over, I made my way to my assigned cabin. I found it had an electric heater with its own thermostat. The best sight was two empty beds and nice thick mattresses. No suitcases on the floor. No clothes on hangers. No roommate!

I unrolled my down sleeping bag on top of the bed closest to the heater, unpacked my clothes and said a silent thank you to the Angels. I didn't believe they had anything to do with my private room, of course, but my thanks were a little ritual I'd fallen into since the Angels interjected themselves into my life. Maybe I started thanking them because I had successfully managed the sole responsibility of three kids and a house. Having the Angels around felt reassuring, as if I had someone on my side and wasn't alone. Still, I didn't believe Angels actually pulled any strings for me—not for a minute.

I sat on my bed and smoked another cigarette then made my way back to the lodge and to the lower room, which wasn't a basement as I'd expected. It too had floor-to-ceiling windows on its longest wall, revealing the lake and snow-covered mountains. Roughly a hundred folding chairs were arranged in a semi-circle around a single-bed mattress—just like the one in my cabin—that lay on the floor in front of a slightly raised platform.

The room was beginning to fill. To cut the chance of having to sit between two people who were ill or dying, I chose a chair at the end of a row. As yet I'd not spotted anyone who appeared sick or dying, but I was taking no chances. Probably the ill patients would be in a room off stage, brought out later to tell their stories and then be hustled away while Dr. Kübler-Ross explained how we were to relate to them.

I noticed a woman being carried around by a young blonde man. She looked normal from her hips up, but her legs were the size of a toddler's. Not a candidate for my dinner table, I decided.

She sat in the center of the front row; I sat three rows back near the windows. The blonde young man and others with her seemed extra cheerful—raised voices, shiny faces, all smiles and giggles. I wondered what they found so amusing; what was wrong with them? Were they morbid? Did they enjoy meeting people who were sick or damaged? Did it make them feel kinder, helpful, or just lucky?

I stepped out on the deck for a cigarette.

As if having to watch a grown woman who wore child-sized shoes on unusable feet but still acted normal and cheerful wasn't odd enough, I found a mimeographed song booklet on my chair when I returned. Were we expected to sing? Singing was an activity I did not do! Not since second grade when my teacher humiliated me by asking me to move my lips but make no sound during the Christmas program.

I made a decision: I was not going to be a happy camper singing happy camping songs. No way.

Dr. Kübler-Ross, the tiny take-me-for-a-tour-woman, entered with two individuals she introduced as staff members Sheila and David. They all sat on the floor at the edge of the raised platform. Sheila made announcements about bathroom locations and the schedule. Then the small woman said, "My name is not Dr. Kübler-Ross, it is Elisabeth. If you call me Dr. Kübler,

Dr. Ross or Dr. anything it will cost you five dollars on the spot." The audience laughed. "You think I joke," she said. "Try it and you will see. Now, we sing."

After fifteen minutes of silly, sad, and familiar songs including "This Little Light of Mine" and "You Are My Sunshine," Elisabeth spoke in an unusual lilting rhythm, perhaps a common accent of people born in Switzerland who learn English as a second language. I don't know. What I do know is that her voice was gentle and sweet. I wanted to catch every syllable.

She didn't lecture. She told stories of her childhood. She told of not being held as a child because there wasn't enough room on her parents' laps for triplet babies. She told of not being recognized as different from her two sisters.

She explained how it felt to fool teachers and boyfriends because no one could tell the triplets apart. How sad it was to be one of three and never one of one. How disappointed she was when her first love couldn't distinguish her from her sisters. She told about the one creature that knew her, never mixed her up with her sisters—her black bunny. And how her father raised rabbits for food, and he made her carry the rabbits to the butcher to be killed and dressed. How the day came when there was only one bunny left and she had to carry her black bunny to the butcher.

Now I understood why there were boxes of tissues at every other seat. Tears and near tears connected everyone in the room. I felt a swelling in my chest and thought surely I would explode if I didn't get away. How was I to manage four more days of this?

Elisabeth announced a physiological break, her term for going pee. I bolted for the stairs along with others and had a lighted cigarette in hand before I cleared the door. Never had I been moved like this, not even at tent revivals in Kentucky where I grew up, where evangelists pleaded for us to come to Jesus. Back then I'd hang onto my chair, white knuckled, for fear I'd walk to the front and be prayed over.

My head reeled: what was happening? Why was I here? I didn't know it was going to be like this. I'm a professional counselor. I can't be crying in front of people. Angels, what have you gotten me into this time?

From the deck outside, I watched the people inside and the staff in particular. They puzzled me. They were different. Even without their badges, it was easy to tell they weren't conference participants. They seemed to radiate warmth, as if some of the sun's heat, that had tanned their skin, remained inside. And even now, after that intense session, the staffers seemed to flow through the room, sliding around obstacles like salmon navigating the shallows of the Anchor River, smooth, graceful, but purposeful. They looked comfortable, at home in this strange place surrounded by strangers.

*

"Stand and tell us who you are and why you are here," Elisabeth said after the break, pointing to a woman in the first row. Gone were the smiles and polite remarks strangers say to one another when forced to sit so close their elbows touch.

A prayer-meeting stillness fell on the room and, like in church, I feared being judged. What was I to say when my turn came? Nix the Angel stuff; this was neither the time nor the place for that disclosure. I had no alternative. I would need to lie.

The woman in the front row stood and spoke. "My name is Agatha. I'm a nun. Mother Superior sent me because I survived breast cancer six years ago. Now it's back. I don't want more treatments and she thinks that's a bad decision and that I'm depressed. But I've prayed about it and I don't want chemo this time. I guess I'm here to please Mother Superior." In jeans and sweater, she didn't look like a nun, and she didn't look ill. Weren't cancer patients bald and thin?

Next, a woman with a Kewpie-doll face introduced herself as Corrine. "I don't know why I came. It's not like I'm sad or anything. I've gotten used it. Ten years ago, my husband took off from Kodiak Island Airfield in his Super Cub and didn't come back. Neither he nor his plane were seen again. Nothing. Just didn't come home. They searched, of course, but didn't find so much as a scrap of fabric. Wouldn't you think something would've washed up if he'd gone down in the ocean? My daughter paid for me to come. Don't know what she expects to change. Nothing's going to bring him home." I thought it odd that she didn't shed a tear. Her voice was flat. She seemed almost as if she was bored.

I agreed with her, what was the point? After all, it had been ten years.

"My name's Peter, I'm a doctor. I work with children who have cancer." He spoke in a soft soprano that I would have mistaken for a woman's voice had I not seen his lips move. He talked about research, new drugs, and his recent divorce. Children with cancer, how awful! Children dying—so unfair—what a waste, I thought. I glanced at the lake and felt I too was filled with icy water. I longed for a cigarette to warm me, to fill my lungs with soothing warm smoke.

"My name is Joanne. My husband and son, Jamie, attended the LDT workshop in California. Jamie asked me to tell you hi, and would you please help his Mommy be happy again." She began crying. She didn't sob or cover her face. She sat still, head held high and spoke evenly as tears met on her chin and dripped onto her purple wool sweater. "How can I be happy when I'm so worried about him? He's only six and all the tests . . ."

"I had seven deaths in one year . . ."

"I lost my wife and two children in an accident last year. . ."

"My child died of cancer two years ago . . ."

"I've been diagnosed with a tumor . . ."

Guilt plugged my ears. What right did I have to sit with these people? What right did I have to hear their stories? My reason for being here was trivial. I burned with shame. What was I to say when it came my turn? I had no courage to tell any lie that would admit me into this group of people who truly suffered. Then, my friend and co-counselor spoke. "Hi, my name's Art. I work with addicts whose losses include many of the same ones mentioned here, including being victims of a terminal illness." He sat down.

It was my turn. "Hi, my name's Jan. I work with him."

*

That night in my cabin, I dreamt I was on a beach, much like the beach in Southern California where I'd lived a lifetime ago. I stood with legs spread in a batter's stance and felt the weight of the baseball bat in my hand. I looked down and saw a brand name circled and burned into its blond wood—DENIAL.

One at a time, baseballs flew toward me. Each had a word inscribed on it: Jesse. Guilty. Home. There were others but I couldn't read them all. I swung the bat and sent each baseball sailing miles out into the ocean.

I woke trembling. My eyes stung for want of tears. In the dark, I fumbled on the floor by my bed and found my cigarettes and the empty Pepsi-can I used for an ashtray. In the dark, I smoked and wondered, What the hell was that about?

CHAPTER THREE
Coats of Many Colors

ONLY 4:30 A.M. and the sun was already up. Alaska's all-day winter darkness was quickly shifting toward summer's near-endless light.

I grabbed my jacket and slipped naked feet into shoes. No time for socks or laces, my bladder insisted. The wooden pathway bounced underfoot as I trotted to the toilets, located with the showers in a separate building halfway to the lodge. I wondered what participants from the lower forty-eight and abroad thought of walking to toilets and showers separated from their rooms when the outside temperature was the usual forty degrees of our Alaska spring.

Breakfast wasn't until 6:30. I dressed, sat on my bed and smoked. This workshop was not a pleasant break from my hectic schedule and tyrant boss Mr. Barnes. My lower back ached. My neck was stiff. Dang those folding chairs! Three more days and I'd qualify for disability. Maybe I should call my gentle Jeff and have him meet me at the road. I could be out of here before breakfast and home in fifteen minutes. Who'd know?

Art would. As my clinical supervisor, he'd be honor-bound to tell the boss. I'd probably get fired. Mr. Barnes had been looking for an excuse to be rid of me since the first day he became director. Though Barnes sent me and Art to the workshop to learn how to handle death and dying issues with our clients, I'd really come to this workshop to talk to Dr.—oops—Elisabeth, about Angels. To leave now would be wasted effort, and besides I'd promised her a tour tomorrow.

Although I lived only seven miles away, I felt as if I'd been transported to a different continent. Yesterday I realized that my accent was the odd one among dialects that were German, British, Australian, Southern U.S., New York, New Jersey, and Connecticut. That's not the only thing about me that seemed out of place, even though I was virtually home. From my seat in the third row I saw an array of bright shirts and tunics in colors like a painter's palette. I'd never seen so many colors of clothing. Everyone looked so clean and pressed. I felt drab and conspicuous in my jeans and much-washed sweatshirt; and their stories were as vivid as their clothes—death, illness, desertion, violence, even murder.

I'd had no pain in my life. I was not a tragic figure. I only knew three people who had died. Grandpa went twenty years ago. No big deal. He was old. It was his time. Then there was Sis's baby, Rosalie, who died when she was nine months old, though I hadn't really known her, only met her once and that was the day we buried her. I remember how strange I'd felt, not sad but more like I had no emotion at all. I'd worried that there was something wrong with me; my baby niece dead and I felt nothing?

Well, then there was Jesse, my high-school sweetheart and first husband. True, he'd been important to me once, but that was ten years ago. I didn't even cry when Mom told me he'd drowned while scuba-diving. No, he didn't matter now.

A shadow of pain crept into my head. That weird beach dream flashed across my mind— the bat, Jesse, the bat, Jesse. More pain. Caffeine withdrawal. My watch told me it was almost 6:30. Surely the coffee was on at the lodge by now.

*

The dining room was bright, warm, moist and marinated in coffee. I cradled a thick, pottery mug, letting it warm my hands when my colleague, Art, entered the dining room. Although dog-sledding was his passion, he looked more like a cowboy, tall and lean. He moved like a loosely strung marionette, feet first, lifted from the knees; then his head and shoulders dragged his flat, skinny butt along. His slow ways and drawl reminded me of my lovable Uncle Clyde and my Kentucky childhood home in Appalachia. At work Art was my rock, the one person who told me I was doing a good job. I didn't always believe his evaluation, but it didn't matter because he was always there to guide me.

We both knew my only qualification for the position of addictions counselor was life experience: I was a refugee from a violent ten-year marriage to an alcoholic. Next month I would graduate from a trade school called A.N.T.I. with twenty-one college credits and an Alcoholism Counselor certificate.

Addiction treatment was an emerging field in the early 1980s, and it was unregulated. If you were an ex-drunk or, like me, the ex-wife of a drunk, that was all you needed to be hired as an addictions counselor.

Alaskan courts had created a demand for counselors, when treatment in lieu of jail time for repeat DUI (Driving Under the Influence) offenders became law. Alaska ranked highest in the nation for deaths associated with alcohol consumption, and programs for alcoholism became the gold rush of the 1980s. Treatment centers sprang up like fireweed in spring.

Quality of treatment varied. Most programs hired only ex-drunks who preached the Alcoholics Anonymous (AA) doctrine. Many programs and practitioners considered psychiatry an enemy to sobriety and said medication of any kind was taboo. Addicts were simply told, "Don't drink, read the AA Big Book, attend meetings, call a friend, find a Higher Power, Let Go and Let God, and recite the Serenity Prayer. This will cause you to have a spiritual awakening and you will stay sober; you will be in recovery." This approach worked for some, but not for all.

The treatment addicts received at the center where I worked was more progressive and went beyond AA. Harold, the Council's first director, had a vision. He believed in combining AA principles with the mental health approach—individual and family counseling—because he recognized that family dynamics played a part in the addiction drama and that there were additional victims besides the drinker. For that reason he hired some staff from outside the AA community. The Council was the first treatment center in the state to have a family therapy program, and I was that program's first and sole employee.

Harold told me and the Board of Directors: "Changing the dynamics of the home environment is essential to the success of our treatment program. If we educate spouses about alcoholism it will raise our success rate." But I knew it was more than that. I needed a job and Harold created the family counseling job for me. Not only did I love my job, I needed it. I had three kids to support.

Why I was offered the job initially was a dirty little secret known only to me and Harold. I guarded it with the fervor of an addict hiding his need. Mr. Barnes and Art didn't know the details of my hiring, and I worried Barnes would discover a secret that fueled my strict professionalism. I dressed better, attended more workshops, read more books, made more public speeches than any other counselor within fifty miles. I never missed an opportunity to speak at schools or civic meetings.

My monthly lectures at the minimum security prison played to standing room only. I knew it wasn't only thirst for knowledge that packed in the inmates; my short skirts, blonde hair and good legs were the draw. Most of the men saw a woman only on visitors' day.

Community visibility was the reason my new boss didn't fire me. I was Ms. Alcoholism Education and Prevention for Wasilla, Palmer, and adjacent communities—and I was a sparkly, blue-eyed blonde with a following.

What would Art do if he knew I'd been at the workshop because of Angel writings?

*

It happened during my first year with the Angels when the dark days of November were upon us. One evening I answered my door to Gloria, a slim, disheveled woman who seemed scared. I'd seen her at Al-Anon meetings (12-step program for families and friends of alcoholics) and I'd admired her demeanor, her meticulous appearance and speech, but she bordered on aloof. Because she declined all invitations to go for coffee after meetings, I didn't know her well enough to understand why she was at my door in this condition or at such a late hour.

I took her coat and sat her down at the dining room table.

I was at the stove making tea when my arm began to tingle, and I glanced over at Gloria. She was staring into space; her fingers worked the top button of the man's plaid shirt she wore over her jeans. The large diamond in her wedding ring flashed in the full-spectrum light from the chandelier. No one spoke.

The tingle in my arm approached pain level. Damn, the Angels were going to put me on the spot again. I reached for the yellow legal pad and pen I kept by the table, sat down and watched myself write words. Like always, the Angels didn't dictate what I should put on paper; they wrote it themselves directly through my hand: *Your keys are behind the dryer. He is safe. You are safe. Angels are here.* I turned the pad so Gloria could read the words.

She began to cry. "Good. He's in no condition to drive. But how did you know?"

"I don't know. I can't explain it. Do you want to talk about what's going on?"

Before she could answer, my hand wrote the Angels' next words: *His secret is death. It is time. Love still lives. Silence brings death. Angels are love.* Then they drew their signature flower—four petals, a stem and two leaves, made in one stroke without lifting the pen from the paper—a scribble. [Note: the drawing at the chapter headings is the actual one taken from Leota's recovered yellow pages.]

12-20-79

this is the lesson for the evening.
it concerns the healing powers of love.
The love energy makes all things
whole. The love of self is the first
law of health in soul. One must
love self before one can love others
or God.
         (the flower is a signature
          they use often.)

A page of Leota's angel writings.

"But I can't tell anyone," she said, sobbing. "He'll lose his job."

I got the tissues, then returned to the yellow pad. *It's time. You don't know what's best. He has a job to do. You don't get to decide. Angels are love.*

"What does that mean?" Gloria asked.

"I don't know. The message is meant for you. I've learned not to interpret." I felt the fool. "What I think is nonsense often turns out to be important to the intended receiver."

Perhaps she'd come to see me because she'd heard about my Angels, but I hated that the Angels just barged in whenever they chose and I had to try to explain their words. Or not explain, as was usually the case. "Please, don't take any of this seriously. If it helps and seems to apply, think about it. Look at it like a third opinion. I don't know who these Angels are or where they come from."

The pen moved again. Lesson of the day: *strong desire at time of death becomes obsession in next life. He died of thirst. Not evil. Know this. Angels are love.* Then they drew a line across the page with such force it cut through three pages. The pen went dead and my hand became my own again.

She read the page several times while I added honey to my lukewarm chamomile. As I stirred my tea, she folded the yellow Angel pages to the size of a coaster, creased the folds with her nail and set her teacup on top of them. She squared her shoulders and seemed to gain more control with each word she spoke. I knew I'd never forget the Angel's words, even though the pages were no longer mine.

Harold, Gloria's husband, had an important job with the city—meaning nearby Anchorage, the biggest city in Alaska—but at home he locked himself in the basement daily and drank until he passed out. His secret drinking defined their twenty-year marriage: he drank, she made excuses and felt responsible. When he became violent she would leave the house, but tonight she hadn't been able to find her keys and had fled in his car. Harold was left at home, but according to the Angels he was without access to a vehicle because her keys were behind the dryer. She offered no explanation as to how she found my house.

Gloria stayed with me for three days, waiting until Harold was committed to a twenty-eight day rehab treatment facility in Anchorage and it was safe for her to return home. Harold lost his job but later became the first director of the Mat-Su Council on Alcoholism and Drug Abuse. Six months later, due to an unstable housing market, the plumbing company where I worked as an accountant shut its doors. It fell to me to pack up the inventory and get it moved into storage. I packed, taped, and worried. How was I to support my family when businesses were closing daily?

As if summoned, in walked Harold, who asked me to come work at the Council. I would work full-time three weeks a month and attend the Alaska Native Training Institute (ANTI) the fourth week. ANTI was a program that taught one subject: alcoholism. On my first day, I discovered I was the only non-native student— the only white face in the school.

So began my career as an addictions counselor. My sorrow was that Harold lost his grip on sobriety before my first year was out. Though given several chances to re-enter treatment, he refused. Mr. Barnes, his replacement, was hired from the lower forty-eight. He seemed to hate me on sight. Art said it was because to Mr. Barnes—himself a recovering alcoholic—I symbolized the non-drinking spouse.

Talk of psychological dynamics was taboo at the Council now that Harold was no longer in charge. So Art and I were misfits both at the Council and in the addiction treatment world. He had a master's degree in psychology; I represented the co-dependent spouse-martyr-punching-bag ready to learn any tactics useful to help other co-dependents. It was a wonder that Art managed to get the Council to fund our participation at the LDT conference where I now sat baffled and amazed.

CHAPTER FOUR

Phone Books and Hoses

DURING THE FIRST MORNING'S breakfast
hour, I watched Art fill a travel-cup with coffee
and amble out the door. It was our secret that
before the morning session he rushed home to
feed his fifteen sled dogs; his wife fed them at
night. LDT workshop rules stated no one was
to leave the grounds, but dogs had to be fed,
daughters had to get to school, and wives had
to work. Even though I covered for him, and
trusted him, I was glad Art didn't know I'd been
hired because the Angels wrote "Your keys are
behind the dryer."

I refilled my coffee cup and wondered what the Angels had in mind for me now. To work with ex-drunks was one thing, but to work with dying people? I worried that the Angels wanted to chat about the afterlife and make all sorts of promises—golden streets and such. I was determined not to be a part of that Angel conversation, arm pain or no arm pain. I'd take drugs before I'd let that happen.

While the other participants sang, I surveyed the room. The boxes of tissues were no longer a mystery, but what about the stack of phone books by the mattress? Sheila, Elisabeth's assistant, announced group rules: no one was to leave the room without getting an okay from a staff member; we weren't to touch or comfort others or offer them tissues; no talking while others were on the mattress—which she called "the mat". We were to stay quiet with our own feelings.

The hair on my arms stood erect. What were we about to experience?

"Who's ready to work?" Elisabeth asked.

No one moved. Silence filled the room. Fear gripped my belly and I grabbed the edges of my chair. What was I afraid of? I wasn't here to work. I was here to observe and learn. With that realization, my hands let go and I relaxed behind the label of professional observer.

Joanne, the California woman whose child had cancer, shifted in her chair. Elisabeth pointed to the mattress and said, "Come, sit on the mat. Tell us why you're here."

Yesterday Joanne wore a purple wool sweater. Today she wore a luscious red one that complemented her gold and diamond jewelry. She knelt on the mat and Elisabeth asked her to remove her rings, watch, and the long chain around her neck. Never as a counselor had I asked clients to remove their jewelry. What in the world was Elisabeth going to make this poor woman do? Gymnastics?

One hundred sets of eyes watched Joanne slip off her wedding rings. She unbuckled her leather watchband and laid it beside the rings on the mat. Reaching under her shoulder-length hair, she unhooked the gold pendant around her neck and latched it again before handing all her jewelry to Sheila. She asked Sheila to be extra careful with the necklace (the tiny prayer-box pendant) because the prayer box held her son's first baby tooth. "He lost it just last month," she added.

The woman sitting next to me pulled a tissue from the box at her feet. I exhaled and longed for a taste of nicotine.

"Jamie has a brain tumor," Joanne began. "At first, I thought he had a touch of the flu or an ear infection. He didn't want to eat and cried a lot. But when I found him in his bed banging his head against the wall, I got scared. The doctor told me it was migraines. But the CAT scan found a tumor."

Joanne sobbed. Snot dripped off her nose. Why didn't Elisabeth give her a tissue? Wasn't she supposed to help Joanne feel better? Why did she just sit there?

No one moved. No sound except Joanne's sobs. It was as if all, except Joanne, were playing the children's game of Freeze. I wanted to scream, "Help her, tell her something to make her feel better!"

Elisabeth sat, elbow on her knee, chin resting in her cupped hand, and watched. She wasn't watching casually. This act of watching seemed to occupy all her senses, her soul. She was one-hundred percent present in her watching.

Joanne stopped mid-sob and looked Elisabeth in the eye. Almost in a whisper Elisabeth asked, "What did you feel when the doctor said Jamie had a brain tumor?" I felt I'd taken a blow. How could Elisabeth ask that question of this mother? I was sure that was wrong. Cruel.

Joanne's head snapped back. Her face flushed and she spat, "I was pissed." Elisabeth slid a phonebook in front of Joanne and laid down what looked like a two-foot length of fat rubber hose, a dark red snake.

"Put it out here," Elisabeth said and smacked the phonebook. I was unprepared for the loud crack of hose hitting the book. I felt I'd been struck and knocked breathless. Where there had been stillness in the room there was now movement. Chairs scraped as they moved backwards, away from the front of the room, away from the violence of this one-hundred-twenty-five pound woman attacking phone books with a hose.

Wordlessly, Elisabeth stacked more books in front of Joanne. Pages flew through the air as Joanne brought the hose high over her head and slammed it down repeatedly.

"Out loud," Elisabeth urged.

"You bastards, what have you done to my baby?" Joanne shouted. "You lied. You said it was a food allergy. You said it was an infection. You lied. Do something!" Each word was paired with a loud whack as hose connected with phonebook. Each time she hit the books my stomach contracted. If she didn't stop soon I would vomit. Why didn't someone make her stop! My head was pounding; I felt sick. I hadn't signed on for anything like this. Angels, damn you!

Finally, the pounding stopped. Joanne sat back on her heels with the hose across her knees. She stared down at the ripped and torn pages scattered about her. She looked limp. I heard sniffles and coughs, and the air was thick with uncertainty. We were held frozen. I didn't dare look around the room; I kept my eyes on Joanne.

She began to talk. About how ashamed she felt when people stared at Jamie's swollen face. How she wanted to tell them it was the medications, that she didn't beat him. She didn't take him shopping anymore because she couldn't stand the looks. She even wished it were someone else's child who was sick. Why did it have to be Jamie? What had she done to deserve a kid with a brain tumor? Venom spilled from her lips; gone was the deceptively sweet wisdom and acceptance she had slung about yesterday. Today her words rang of truth.

I cried.

Joanne spoke of wanting to run away and leave Jamie with his dad, David. How she hated that David could laugh with Jamie. How angry she was that she had to quit her job to take care of Jamie, while David could go to work each day and have a normal life. Joanne folded forward, head on the mat, and cried. It was a different cry than before, more a loud wail. The grating sound of tissues ripped from boxes and noses blowing played backup for her solo. Elisabeth sat and listened.

Oh my God, I thought, I can't stand a week of this. People pay money for this?

I glanced at Sheila. She had the ghost of a smile hidden behind a solemn expression. She stood and announced a fifteen-minute break.

*

So went the day. More stories, more sounds that felt like assaults. By the evening meal break, no coherent thought traversed my synapses. My brain was numb, my heart locked in a vault. No more! I was past compassion or even interest; all I wanted was escape. I skipped dinner and limped to my cabin for silence and solitude.

Seeking distraction, I tried to read the Martha Grimes mystery novel I'd brought along. No luck, brain wouldn't cooperate. For comfort, I laid out my crystal collection. As I fondled each stone, a different friend's face or an event appeared, reminding me of how each crystal came into my possession. But when I touched my most recent gift, a small quartz crystal, I heard a jeering little voice in my left ear: *That doesn't belong to you. It's Elisabeth's.*

I argued, "It's a gift!"

It doesn't belong to you. It belongs to Elisabeth! The Angel vocally stamped its foot.

"Pat gave me this. She would be hurt if I gave it away."

It isn't yours. You can't keep what isn't yours.

But it was mine; it was a special gift from my dear friend Pat who believed in my Angel voices even when I tried not to believe in them myself. "She brought it from a healing conference. It's special."

It is not yours!

"I won't give it away. It was a gift!"

I rolled shut my blue-satin traveling jewel-case. I'd sought comfort but had found anger, and it boiled in my stomach. My doctor had diagnosed my frequent abdominal pains as nervous stomach. "Pre-ulcer," he'd said.

I lay on my bed in the dark and smoked. If I couldn't see the crystal pouch, I wouldn't hear the Angels. I'd had all I could tolerate for one day. I wanted sleep. I wanted peace. I wanted to go home.

CHAPTER FIVE

A Moose-Horn Ring

I WOKE THE NEXT MORNING after a fitful night's sleep and wondered how I'd get through the day. I couldn't think clearly. My pre-ulcer stomach felt raw. It cramped when I moved, and coffee was but a wishful thought. Scummy teeth, cigarette breath, and body odor decreed day three as Shower-Day.

With bare necessities rolled inside my towel, I pulled on my coat and bounced down the walkway to the showers, best described as primitive. A damp, dark hall with a slotted bench bolted to the cement wall was the dressing area. If something needed to stay dry, it had better be on one of the hooks above the bench because all else was wet. Naked women, some faces I recognized from the conference, passed one another to and from the showers.

I entered a large cement room better suited for a prison: showerheads on all four walls and a hubcap-sized drain in the center of the slanted floor; no stalls, no curtains, no tile on the rough cement floors. Even high-school showers had curtained stalls! Hot water spraying the cold walls and floor filled the room with steam.

Teeth chattering, damp and miserable, I returned to my cabin, blow-dried my hair and dressed in jeans and a clean sweatshirt. Dry clothes and curled hair transformed the forty-degree morning into a feeling of summer, so instead of my usual hurried pace, I strolled to the lodge, thinking maybe, just maybe, I'd survive the week intact. Do you hear that, Angels? I will survive!

I surrendered my body again to a hateful folding chair and wondered what Elisabeth expected to see on our tour planned for the after-lunch break, so instead of wondering how the mother of a murdered child could ever feel joy or love again, I wondered if the Hatcher Pass Road was firm enough for us to make it to the abandoned mine at the top. The drive was less than twenty miles but was a steady, uphill climb on a narrow road. In many places it was wide enough for only one car, and its curves were all blind. We wouldn't get out of the car at the top because the rotting snow would be over our shoes, but the view was one hundred percent Alaska: immense, rugged, and wild.

I could think of no other choice for the tour. I was sure Elisabeth wasn't interested in the experimental farm where scientists tried to invent crops that could flourish in Alaska's ninety-day growing season of cool temperatures and constant daylight. Some crops, like corn, wouldn't mature without darkness. Broccoli, cauliflower, pumpkins, and cabbage were the most popular crops in our area. Was Elisabeth interested in agriculture? I doubted it. She might like to visit the musk ox farm, but that was too far to drive. Hatcher Pass would have to do.

I was preoccupied as the parade of angry, frightened, or sad individuals made their way to the front of the room to sit on the mat. I heard the noise and saw the tears, but their pain didn't reach into me as it had yesterday. The morning passed and Sheila announced lunch.

Unconcerned for others, I pushed ahead of the crowd to be first at the only pay-phone in the lodge. "Elisabeth said she'd be ready by one o'clock," I told Jeff. "You can bring the car now."

Outside on the porch I smoked a cigarette before heading for the buffet line. The food was uninteresting, and I finished quickly. While bussing my plate at the kitchen sink, I heard Elisabeth make an announcement that ended with the word *ring*.

It's yours, an Angel buzzed into my ear.

Can't be, I didn't bring rings.

It's yours. Go look!

Stop it. I didn't bring any jewelry with me.

Just go look. What will it hurt to look?

Then, over my other shoulder, a male voice said, "Elisabeth has your ring." I spun and bumped into my gentle Jeff's camouflaged chest. He always dressed in the unofficial uniform of the wounded Vietnam vet. Like so many others, his wounds were not visible, nor had they earned him a purple heart, but he was nonetheless a wounded soldier.

He repeated, "Elisabeth has your moose-horn ring. She just announced it." I tried to argue, but he shoved me through the kitchen doors into the dining room.

In the center of the room, Elisabeth stood on top of a table, her arm extended high above her head. In her hand she held a ring. I approached and she asked, "This is yours?" I must have nodded because she handed it over. "Someone found it in the shower this morning." She climbed down from the table.

"But you don't understand," I sputtered. "I didn't bring this ring with me." I tried to explain it couldn't be my ring because I'd lost mine at home the night before the workshop. Yet, as I protested, I recognized the crude, not-so-round circle of moose-horn in my palm. I fingered bumps and scratches left there by a knife in the hand of an unskilled ten-year-old. Jeff had helped Travis make the ring for my forty-second birthday.

Elisabeth patted my shoulder and said, "Yes, your Guides help you with things like that." Without pausing, Elisabeth asked, "Is your car here? We go for tour now?"

My ten-year-old Volvo wore its winter coat of grime. I was embarrassed and mumbled an apology that no one heard while Jeff and the staff-member Sheila climbed into the backseat. At least the inside was neater than I had left it. Jeff had removed the trampled homework papers and other child-created debris from the floor, and he'd emptied the ever-overflowing ashtray.

Elisabeth, in the front seat, tilted her head toward the crystal sphere that hung from the rearview mirror. "Is that so your Guides can direct you? Or just because it is a pretty thing?"

"No... Yes... Sort of... Both, I guess."

"So it is because your Guides use it to communicate with you and it is pretty?"

"Sort of..." When signing up for the LDT, I'd written to her in vague terms about my Angels and my desire to know if they were spirit guides or a product of my imagination. Now I tried to discount my disclosure, but I was no match for her clear-eyed curiosity. My Angels were outed.

I turned right at the junction and headed up into Hatcher Pass. It rose high enough, but was an infant in the family of snow-blanketed mountains that comprised the lodge's majestic view. As we climbed, Elisabeth asked, "Do you know why I come back to Alaska? It is because it reminds me of my beloved Switzerland. The mountains! The air! Out of the cities one can breathe."

She lit a cigarette. On her exhaled smoke came her explanation that smoking didn't need to be harmful as long as one took care of "unfinished business." That was the best news I'd heard in a decade, and she was a doctor! I lit up and made a note to learn more about "unfinished business" and to take care of mine, if I had any. "So... tell me more about these adorable Angels," she said.

"I don't know where to start."

"At the beginning."

I told her about Betty and the Ouija board. How, through my hand, the Angels wrote messages on my yellow pad, and I was expected to deliver the messages, often to strangers. I had no choice but to approach people I didn't know and hand them messy scribbled letters signed "Angels." I told Elizabeth how if I didn't deliver the letters, the Angels wrote the same phrases over and over whenever my hand held a pen to paper, even when I tried to write checks. It seemed she had come because she'd heard about my Angels but I hated that the Angels just barged in whenever they chose and I had to try and explain their words.

The pavement ended, and I slowed the car until I was sure the dirt road was firm. It was a bit soft but it held.

"How long have you been writing for these Angels?" Elisabeth asked.

"Two years. But how do I know if it's Angels or me? What if I'm just making it all up? And if I'm not, why me? I'm not even religious."

"Maybe that is why," she said.

"What?" I jerked the car hard right to avoid a deep rut in the center of a curve. I think Sheila's head hit the window.

The dirt road was quickly disappearing under our tires, but Elisabeth continued talking as if we were on dry pavement instead of brown mush. "If you were religious you would expect a burning bush or a bleeding statue, not Angels writing letters. See? Like that."

"But what if it's my unconscious? Maybe I just want attention."

"Do you want attention?"

"Well, not this kind."

Hatcher Pass in early May had been a bad idea. I hoped to find a spot wide enough and dry enough for turning around.

"They write for you, no? Tell you things to help you?"

"Not really. I've tried a few times—my hand wants to move, but it doesn't, so I don't try anymore. But they talk to me. It's usually one certain voice in my left ear. The first time it happened I thought someone behind me was speaking."

"What do they tell you?"

"They told me you had my ring at lunch today. Stuff like that. When extraordinary things happen they take the credit, claim they made them happen. Like me attending this workshop." The back end of the Volvo lost traction and we slipped sideways on a steep incline. Angels, if I ever needed you to be real, this is it. Find us a turnaround.

"Goot. You come tomorrow and see if Angels have something for me."

Around the next curve, the road leveled out where there was a well-graveled wide spot. I held my breath and edged onto the gravel. There was barely enough room to maneuver between the mountain on one side and empty air on the other. I had to inch forward and backward several times before I got the car headed back down the mountain. Elisabeth seemed not to notice, but I could feel Jeff's hand gripping the back of my seat and taste his wish to be in the driver's seat.

We got back to the lodge with time to spare before the afternoon session was to start. Elisabeth and I went to our respective rooms, leaving Sheila and Jeff in the parking lot talking.

What? Jeff and Sheila talking? But Jeff didn't talk to anyone.

CHAPTER SIX
A Little Red Dress

THE SONG "This Little Light of Mine" ended the warm-up for afternoon session. Elisabeth asked, "Who's ready to work?"

Albert—a mild-mannered German gentleman seated beside me—stood, stepped over my legs, and shuffled to the front. Without removing his shoes, he knelt on the clean sheet that replaced the tear-stained one of yesterday. Weathered brown hands took up the hose casually, like a familiar tool, and without hesitation Albert started to hammer the phonebooks.

Gone was my ability to distance myself; I was once again present in this bizarre room filled with violence. Albert's dark features were so like those of my ex-husband's when they were contorted in anger. I felt nauseous. He cursed some absent woman, called her bitch, cunt—words familiar to me, especially when wedded to anger and violence. Elbows on knees, hands over my ears, I absorbed each of his blows. Old wounds opened. I felt bruised and sore. His words made me the size of a cowering five-year-old. Tears washed my face.

When the noise stopped, I glanced up to see a trembling Albert curled around a pillow he held crushed to his chest. He was sobbing into it. After his spasms quieted he told of childhood sexual abuse suffered at the hands of an older cousin. I felt like Carrie in that horrible movie as his shame spilled over me.

I should have been bleeding. I should have wrapped my legs around my chair like in grammar school. Maybe then I would have remained in my seat. I wouldn't have shot out of my chair and taken a place in the front of the room with my knees sinking into this mat that felt just like the mattress on the bed in my room at home.

I sat motionless. Memories flashed like photographs in a peep-show. Each one spun me backward in time. First, a fist wearing a wedding band smashed my face and blood sprayed from my nose. Even twenty years later, my mind raced with my remembered excuses: He's drunk. He doesn't know what he's doing. He didn't mean it. I should have had dinner on the table—not in the oven. Next time I'll get it right.

Spinning and swirling pictures of forgotten scenes flooded my vision: a campus at night, six young men, taunting and insulting, rough stucco scratching through my thin summer blouse, hands squeezing budding breasts and grabbing at my crotch, car lights sweeping the building, the gang running off; an embossed album of wedding pictures flipped by and slammed shut on a divorce decree; the image of a once-favorite red sundress, with teasing spaghetti-strap bows atop nineteen-year-old tan shoulders; hurtful callused hands scorched the inside of my thighs; photo developer and the vinegary odor of stop-bath burned my nose in a photo lab in San Diego. I felt engulfed in a wave of shame so thick it choked off crying for help.

I was lost to the presence of the room filled with people, trapped in my memories of secret sins and shame I had purposely forgotten and promised no one would ever know. Get over it and forget it had been my strategy. Keep on keeping on. Now I was about to unravel and didn't know how to stop.

"Get it out," Elisabeth said.

My arms refused to rise; my hands wouldn't close around the hose. Lot's wife, I might have been, judging from my lack of action. Unlike the other participants who hit and screamed, I couldn't move. "It isn't fair," I whispered, then folded forward and gagged.

"What isn't fair?" Elisabeth asked as she placed a wastebasket in front of me. My façade of professionalism destroyed, I bent forward and retched, flinging globs of white mucus into the pail until nothing was left. "Goot. Under the fear is anger. Get it out." She put the hose into my limp hands again.

"I can't," I said and hated the whiny, sniveling coward that was me.

"Get it out. Finish what you have started."

"I can't." Whack. "No." Whack. "Stop!" Whack. "Stop. Don't touch me. I didn't do anything wrong. You had no right. No, no, no." Tears came and I cried for that naïve girl who didn't know it was dangerous to look pretty. That girl who walked in innocence in new high-heel shoes, swinging her hips and loving the feel of her red skirt as it moved against her thighs and calves. I cried for the girl who thought none of it would have happened if she hadn't worn the red sundress.

I cried for the young wife who tried too hard and stayed ten years with a violent drunk. With help from Elisabeth, I found righteous anger. The metallic taste of it flooded my mouth.

Eighth-grade had been the last time I'd tasted anger; my teacher had pulled me off the fat kid who sat behind me in English class just as he was about to say, "I'm sorry." He'd snapped my bra strap, and I demanded an apology by using his hair as handles to slam his head onto the hood ornament of a black Chrysler. Teacher said I had no right. "Nice girls don't act that way. Nice girls don't get angry."

Now I poured out angry words, drenched myself with tears, slammed the hose against the books—yet my throat was still locked against screaming.

Without words, Elisabeth taught me there's a place for anger in everyone's life, that everyone has a right to be angry when mistreated or violated.

I returned to my seat in a daze and remained so the rest of the day. Others made their way to the front of the room and screamed, cried, or raged as was their need. This time, their sounds no longer assaulted me. I no longer needed them to stop. I'd spent my anger and grief for that day. The cries of others had lost the power to cause me pain.

*

In my cabin that evening, I took inventory of body and mind. No stomach pain, not a twinge. No headache. No aches or pains anywhere, and my thoughts flowed smoothly. What had happened to me on the mat? Why did I feel so different? It was as if all urgency and confinement had been removed. Nothing weighed on me. I felt free. My breath was easy, my body relaxed.

A few years back my father had attended a tent revival and told of being healed by the laying-on-of-hands. I wondered if this was how he'd felt.

But healed? Me? No way. I didn't believe in that nonsense.

Out of nowhere came that aggravating little voice in my left ear: *Tomorrow you will give Elisabeth her crystal.*

I held to my argument. "I told you that crystal was a gift and I'm not giving it away. She'll think I'm nuts." Even as I spoke, I knew that was a lie. Elisabeth was a believer.

You know the rule. You can't keep what isn't yours. Remember what you give away will be returned to you tenfold.

I'd heard that before; it seemed one of their favorite theories. The Angels had a long list of one-liners which they quoted as laws of nature.

CHAPTER SEVEN
A Coincidence of Crystals

SHIFTING TO FIND a soft spot in the hateful folding chair the next morning, my body felt different. Gone were the restrictions in my throat and the twisted knots in my intestines. My stomach was chewing on my oatmeal breakfast instead of its own lining.

I looked around at my companions: no scorecard needed to distinguish those who still held tight to their self-control and those who'd lost their dignity on the mat. The latter were loose-limbed, legs sprawled at odd angles, ankles crossed, arms draped over neighbors' chair-backs or resting in laps. Violence still raged at the front of room, but the veterans of the mat—myself included—were less affected by it.

I listened to the self-hatred of a mother whose son had shot himself, and her story had no power to force my attention outside the room to the glacier-choked mountains behind the lake. I stayed present and heard the depth of her despair. I saw her desire for death flare into flame, visible to all who would see. Elisabeth nudged her, and the mother's anger asserted itself. The hose became the tail of a raging bull and she held tight, screaming incoherent hatred. I rode with her through her rage and into oceanic tears. Her tears, not mine. My eyes were dry and observant. Her sobs, deep in the belly at first, changed tone and meaning as her grief spilled out into the room.

She spoke of missing her son's physical presence, her longing to hold and comfort her child. She said her body and stomach ached with the pain of having to live her life without her eldest child. She mourned her lost opportunity to prevent his death. Gone was her chance to tell him, just once more, how much she loved him. From behind her breastbone came hiccup-sobs for the events she could never share with her child: his eighteenth birthday, his graduation from high school, his wedding, her first grandchild. Her tears wound down until a smile poked at the corners of her mouth as she recalled the day he asked where babies came from and she sent him to his dad for the answer.

I felt I shared a sacred space with this mother, a place from which I could offer support and counsel. It was then I considered Elisabeth's remark on day one of the workshop: "You do not feel the pain of others. You feel only your own pain. Your pain is your unfinished business." I hadn't understood even when she explained, "Put a crying baby in a room of adults and everyone will try to hush the baby. Why? Because the baby's cries push on the reservoir of unshed tears (unfinished business) inside each adult, and this causes them pain. To stop their pain, they try to stop the baby's cries."

I'd had all kinds of excuses why this was not so: the baby might have a messy diaper or be hungry or have a tummy ache, and it's natural for adults to want to help the child. As a mother of three, I knew about crying babies, but now I had to rethink my position.

Yesterday I would have joined this mother in her distress. My stomach would've been in a knot, I'd have been nauseous, would've begged her to shut up. In my helplessness, I'd have promised her that "time would heal" and that "this too shall pass". I might even have said—God forgive me—" "he's in a better place." I would have missed the way she moved from helpless victim through anger and tears to a loving memory that ended with a smile. How did this happen? Could just anyone work Elisabeth's magic? Was there a formula? Could it be learned?

Thursday morning, when we broke for lunch, all but five participants had visited the mat. Unlike the previous days, this session ended with singing. I sang! The atmosphere was light. I half expected to see butterflies or fireflies in the room, except that we were in Alaska in May.

Sheila announced that this ended the working part of the Life, Death, and Transition Workshop. We'd been here four days. Tonight we would celebrate with a ceremony. The participants were to create a ritual to honor our experience and to thank the staff. We would gather at the bonfire by the lake after dinner.

Elisabeth was the last to speak. "There is no death," she said, a phrase she'd repeated every day of the workshop. This time she elaborated on that theme. "I'm a scientist. My research proves there is no death." She went on to tell about being hooked up to measuring devices that proved she had died thousands of times.

How could that be?

She added that we would be able to peruse her research and books at tonight's celebration.

I perked up. Could there be scientific data that proved life after death? At age thirteen I'd insisted on proof, but no preacher or Sunday School teacher could provide any. "You have to have faith," they always said.

Even at thirteen, I thought that believing in life after death without evidence was foolish. Besides, I had bushels of evidence that death was final. My dog Nicky was dead, hit by a delivery van; my grand-dad was dead; all the bunnies, sparrows, and baby mice I'd rescued had died. I hadn't heard a peep or squeak from any of them since. Until I heard from the other side, death was final. That was my stance then, and not much had changed in the interim.

Now I was open to new information that might prove otherwise. Would Elisabeth convince me of life after death when my father, a Pentecostal minister, had not? Would tonight end my search for truth?

*

Instead of working with the others in planning the celebration ceremony, I hid in my cabin, fingered "Elisabeth's" crystal, and decided to put the Angels' theory of ownership to the test. After all, wasn't putting the Angels on trial my reason for being here? How could I accept any verdict if it went untested?

Recalling a phrase my mom often quoted, "Might as well let the tail go with the hide," I put the cloudy quartz crystal, given to me as a healing stone, inside its blue satin bag. I knew it wouldn't matter to Pat if I gave it away, lost it, threw it away, or held it in high esteem. She practiced the Angels' lesson on gifting: A gift given is not truly given until all expectations for care and use are severed.

I could tell my resistance to parting with the crystal stemmed from a desire to increase my crystal collection. Guilt for my greediness pulled at my chest, and a different Angel lesson ran marquee-like through my head: To live guilt free, change either your actions or the way you think about them. The gift of guilt is self-esteem.

I tucked the blue pouch into my jeans pocket and gathered up a couple of pens and the yellow legal tablet I'd brought to the conference. Usually this pad would be filled with numbered theories, starred solutions to problematic situations, bulleted points to present at the staff meeting next Wednesday. Here it was, a blank eleven-by-fourteen billboard that testified how differently this workshop had unfolded from all others I'd attended. How was I to explain to the staff the value of this workshop, how it applied to addiction treatment, why it was worth the money? Like Scarlet O'Hara, I'd "think about that tomorrow."

A special crystal

*

I covered the short distance between my cabin and staff housing quickly and knocked on Elisabeth's door, keeping the appointment she'd made with me during our drive. It opened immediately as if she'd been standing beside it waiting. "I have something of yours," she said without preamble and walked into the adjoining room. Upon her return, she took my hand and placed in it a bulging red satin pouch. "This doesn't belong to me. It's yours."

I couldn't move or speak, just stood looking at my palm. I'm sure my mouth gaped.

"Open it," she urged.

"I have something for you too," I said, digging the blue satin pouch from my jeans pocket. Her expression reminded me of a child's instant and uncensored delight when given a gift. Still standing in the foyer, we opened our gifts and each held up a cloudy quartz crystal, identical in every way except size. The one Elisabeth gave me was easily ten times larger than the one I gave her. We held them side by side. They had the same degree of cloudiness and the exact same number of babies (or barnacles—smaller crystals attached to the sides of larger ones), identical in proportion, placement, and angle of growth. I knew the shape of a natural crystal is dictated by laws of physics but size and clusters are random. A shiver ran through me. Was this coincidence a warning or a promise?

Elisabeth showed me along a dark hallway to a bright sitting room. Like the lodge next door, this room had large windows along the wall that faced the lake. We sat on low chairs with tea, cigarettes, and chocolate. Elisabeth was never far from chocolate—Swiss chocolate, sent to her by her sister Eva. Each time I saw her eat a small square of her chocolate, I felt I was watching her take communion.

I would later learn that American chocolate, or other imported chocolate, she shared generously— but not her Swiss delicacy. Today, as I was a first-time guest, she offered me a small square, but I declined. With tea in one hand, cigarette in the other, and yellow legal pad on my lap, I had no room for chocolate. Besides, I was nervous. What if the Angels wrote something silly or wrong for this psychiatrist whose reputation was global?

Wait a minute. Didn't I want the Angels to fail the examination? Wasn't it my desire to have Elisabeth pronounce them false, merely pranks I used to draw attention to myself? Reduce them to a party trick I could dismiss and ignore? No longer would I suffer the temptation to test their theories ("lessons," the Angels labeled them). Wasn't that my goal? Didn't I spend months imagining how Dr. Elisabeth Kübler-Ross, world famous psychiatrist who communicated with spirit guides and the dead, would rid me of these intrusive voices? Yes!

Or, did I secretly want her to pronounce them real beings from another realm with special knowledge and important information? Did I secretly want her to tell me I was special?

My arm tingled. I took up the pen. *Elisabeth you have followed your path with great courage. Many are grateful. Others have tried to silence your message. You were not distracted.*

I sensed a movement near my right elbow. Elisabeth had squatted inches from the tablet with her eyes on the scribbling that trailed behind my hand. Her focus was such that it suggested those odd lines were all that existed in the room, or in the world. *Your guides are present and they say thank you, you are a good student. You've learned your lessons well even when others did not believe.*

A giggle escaped her small frame, and she swept the room with her eyes but moved not a muscle. How could anyone sit that still? *Jan resists. Say she is to write for the Angels. Angels are love. Mankind needs Angels' lessons on love. Not the romantic love spoken of in movies. Creation love—loving with intent.*

Damn. Why did they have to write that? Now what would I say? I hated it when they started talking about mankind needs this, mankind needs that. It was just too much. I wasn't about to try to tell mankind what it needs or wants.

"This true? You not want to write for these Angels?" Elisabeth asked.

"I don't know who they are, where they come from. What if it's just me, my imagination at play?"

"What is the problem? You say what if it's just me. Then you say you don't write these words. I don't understand. Either you believe the Angels write this. Or you believe you write this."

I flushed and squirmed. I wanted out of this room. Away from this pint-sized foreigner who saw things too simply. The Angels were complicated. Maybe Elisabeth was as unreliable as some skeptical media coverage suggested.

"What if the things they write aren't true?" I asked.

"Do you know of lies?"

"No."

"Again I don't understand."

Pain jabbed my shoulder and shot down my arm. *Not for you to decide. Messages not for you to judge.* The page ripped with the force of the line drawn across it. *Now we speak of energy. Energy for energy is the law. To give energy without equal value is to cause harm. Elisabeth, you have violated this law. You give energy without equal return. Clean this up.*

Oh boy, now I'd done it. So much for Elisabeth understanding it wasn't me when they wrote "You are wonderful and loved." Now they were writing something that suggested Elisabeth was doing something wrong. Now what?

Money is symbol of the energy used to earn it. Money is traded for services of another—energy for energy—balance. Hire one who counts. You are not skilled in this area. Angels are love (signature flower).

The pen fell from my hand and rolled onto the carpet. Elisabeth took the pad and read the message several times. Then she asked if she could keep the pages.

"Sure. They belong to you." As I handed them over, I was sure the message was seared in my brain. I'd never forget those Angel words.

Without further comment, Elisabeth poured more tea. As we sipped, she suggested that I become the Alaska Coordinator for her organization, Shanti Nilaya. The name, she explained, was a Sanskrit phrase which means "the final home of peace." The headquarters were in Escondido, California, and she used the place as a base for workshops, exploring out-of-body experiences and developing new lectures, including one on "Death and Life after Death."

"Sure," I said, assuming the position couldn't involve much work because Elisabeth would probably rarely, if ever, return to Alaska.

Then she asked me, meaning the Angels, to write for her each month and send the pages to her. Since all mail was opened by her secretary, I was to write "personal" on the outside of the envelope.

CHAPTER EIGHT

Three Lovers

ALONE IN MY CABIN that afternoon, I sat on my bed smoking and turning the new crystal over in my hand. I felt deflated, empty. Gone was the hope of being free of the Angels. Gone was the hope that a knowledgeable person, someone I could respect, would declare the Angels a form of mental illness and prescribe me drugs to silence them. Also gone was the hope of hearing, "Yes Jan, you are being visited by messengers of God." Thank the Lord she didn't say that.

She hadn't said anything. I was right where I was before I came to this despicable workshop, except that I'd made a fool of myself on the mat in front of Art.

Shit! Keeping it together at work, always remaining professional, putting on a good act—those were my talents. Looking good covered my lack of knowledge. Looking good supported my family. But Art saw me on the mat. He saw me come unraveled. I'll probably lose my job. Shit... shit... shit. I pounded my pillow then collapsed and cried myself to sleep.

Growling hunger woke me. No jabbering Angels greeted me, which was a relief. My watch promised dinner in half an hour. I rushed to the frigid bathhouse with just enough time to make myself presentable.

Face washed, hair touched up, I tried to sort myself out on the short walk from bathhouse to lodge. What had I lost or gained in these days away from home? I'd met a famous person, although that wasn't something of any lasting benefit. The ring Travis carved for me had been returned, but that came with relief that I didn't have admit to my ten-year-old son that while taking a bath at home, I'd lost a gift he'd been so proud to give me. The downside was that I didn't know how it got into the bathroom at the lodge. I knew it hadn't come with me, rolled in my towel or my underwear; I'd checked those the first day. Yet someone found it and gave it to Elisabeth, who returned it to me! I didn't like things I couldn't explain, including the whole matching crystals episode.

I'd arrived at this workshop wanting answers but it looked like I'd be leaving with more questions. Now Elisabeth wanted me to Angel-write for her every month and mail her the "yellow pages."

Could psychiatrists be kooks?

I was convinced that my job was in jeopardy. I'd been on shaky ground before the workshop. Art hadn't gone on the mat—surely I'd have seen if he had—yet he'd seen me on it acting in such a non-professional manner—in public! He would surely think less of me now. Would he still fight to keep me and the family program?

A young woman joined me now at the ashtray and ruined my perfect score for avoiding contact with other LDT participants—a four-day record. I was someone who typically networked the crowd at every workshop. That's how I'd earned my position as Ms. Alcoholism Education and Prevention, fed my family and paid the mortgage. Here, I was aloof.

She lit a thin, brown cigarette and asked, "What's with the mud, you suppose? It hasn't rained." Her brisk manner fit her blonde-to-white crew cut, black jeans and black leather flight jacket. She was one of the few who'd been taken into a side room to work, so I didn't know anything about her except that her speech said New York.

"Permafrost," I said. "Under the grass and soil are many feet of frozen-solid dirt and rocks. That's the permafrost. It can't absorb the snow-melt, so everything just sits on top and causes havoc until warmer weather makes the permafrost recede a little."

"You live around here?"

"Yeah, down the road about seven miles."

"You like it? With all the mud?"

"I don't like the mud but, yeah, I guess I like it. A woman has more freedom here than in the lower forty-eight where I came from. No one here tells you not to do something. If you think you can do it, people just stand back and watch. I like that." I finished my cigarette, added the butt to the collection in the ashtray, and left her standing and gazing over the near-empty parking lot.

Due to the mud and the outside temperature— fifteen degrees above freezing—the planned celebration by the participants was moved into the group room downstairs, sans the promised bonfire. Others had decorated the room with butterfly cutouts, streamers and candles. The mattresses were gone, the chairs rearranged into short rows, and the stage was set with chairs for

Elisabeth and staff. Best of all, there were no songbooks on the chairs.

Everyone, except Art and me, had dressed in festive clothes, colorful dresses, bright shirts, perfect makeup with painted smiles all round. Art and I looked like refugees in our worn jeans and sweatshirts. We huddled together on the lakeside aisle, and he told me his lead dog was in a slump. Said his daughter was in a music program at school. We whispered other news, and he asked if I'd heard from my kids. No reference to my time on the mat; he was just his normal, pre-workshop self. My heart swelled with gratitude for this man.

The party—its short speeches and special cake—vibrated with gratitude from all of us. The good will was palpable.

*

After breakfast, we gathered for the last time in the downstairs group room where a podium had been placed on stage. Tables along one wall displayed Elisabeth's books along with cassettes and videos of her lectures.

The room quieted when Elisabeth stepped up to the podium. Static grated our ears as she adjusted the microphone. "A position has become available at my beloved Shanti Nilaya. We need accountant. The job requires you go to Southern California. See Sheila after auction to apply."

To say I was shocked would be like saying the 1964 earthquake that destroyed downtown Anchorage and killed hundreds was a tremor. Elisabeth was violating what I'd told her was my number one, iron-clad rule related to Angel writing: Wait and See. Elisabeth wasn't waiting even a day since she'd heard from the Angels that she should hire someone.

Had she been planning to hire an accountant all along? Or did this announcement grow from yesterday's Angel writing that told her "Hire one who counts"? Was she yet another resident of la-la-land who swallowed the writings whole, as if dropped from the lips of God?

I darted outside for a much-needed cigarette.

When I returned to my seat, one of the staffers, David, stepped onto the stage to announce that he was to wear his auctioneer's hat this morning. The room came alive under his skill as he joked and cajoled participants into paying outrageous prices for all manner of things, with proceeds supporting the LDT scholarship fund that made attendance possible for cancer patients and their families. Rainbow scarves hand-knitted by Elisabeth sold for the price of one scholarship. Phonebooks and hoses were sold together as "externalization kits."

The most prized item was a child's toy, a handmade lime-green caterpillar, that—when turned inside out—became a butterfly. Elisabeth used the caterpillar-into-butterfly metaphor in her lectures and books to explain her belief that death is merely a permanent transformation. The twenty-dollar toy sold for over four hundred dollars.

While others contributed hundreds to the scholarship fund, my mind turned to home and the kids. I wondered whose feelings might need to be soothed, what limits needed defending, and if I had alligators to kill at work. I thought of the fun I was going to have telling Pat I'd given away the crystal she gave me and had received a larger, nearly identical one from Elisabeth. Her face would light up and she'd do her little grunt-laugh, then reel off an Angel quote: "Let material possessions flow through your life to be truly open to prosperity." She'd memorized hundreds of these; I don't believe Pat ever forgot a word the Angels wrote in her presence.

The crystal exchange wasn't a story I would tell to just anyone. I sure didn't plan to tell the new man in my life, Jerry. I wanted him to see me as practical and responsible first, and then I'd tell him about the Angels. In the three months we'd dated, I'd come to view Jerry as straight and narrow in some ways, and I was unsure of his religious beliefs because of the mix-up the night we first met.

It had been after the opening performance of the play "A Touch of the Poet," in which I'd played Nora, the female lead. Afterward, the cast and crew went dancing at the Moose Club to celebrate. I noticed a man sitting alone at the bar as soon as we walked in. Tall and lanky, his face tan with cheeks like flat planes, this man had Clint Eastwood good looks. He seemed about my age, 40-ish. The evening unfolded like a scene from the song "Some Enchanted Evening"— eyes meeting across a crowded room. I flirted, smiled when we made eye contact, and danced with every man in the room. I wanted him to know I was available.

He didn't move, just sat watching my crowd of theater friends, and smiling. Meanwhile, the Angels were chattering away in my left ear, feeding me information about him: *He likes you. He's single. He's shy.* Then they switched to nagging: *You'll have to make the first move. Don't let him walk out. He's the one.*

Finally, I got two-drink courage and asked him to dance. We glided onto the floor, and as a conversation opener I asked, "What do you do for a living?"

"I'm a carpenter." My response must have been slow because he continued, "I guess you don't think much of carpenters. Jesus Christ was a carpenter, you know."

I spoke without thinking. "Yes, and you know what they did to him."

End of conversation. We danced on in silence. I was sure I'd blown it, but now, three months later, we were still seeing each other.

I liked Jerry. I liked how I felt in his arms. I wanted a chance to see where this relationship would go. For now I'd keep religion off limits, but that wasn't the only touchy subject. He was a forty-seven-year-old widower whose wife had recently died of cancer. I didn't want to come on too strong. I wanted to be considerate.

It wasn't so much that I wanted to be considerate; it was that I didn't want to screw up. Jerry was the nicest guy I'd dated in years, and my kids liked him too. A down-to-earth straight talker, Jerry was a good person as well as funny in a droll way. The kids and I considered him solid, the kind of man who'd be there when you needed him and would never turn mean or violent. "He'll take care of you, Mom." That would be a quite a change from Jesse, the teacher, my first husband, who'd drowned in a California ocean, and from my second husband, Keith, the batterer.

After my first date with Jerry, Christine, my tall, dark-haired twelve-year-old, cornered me in the kitchen. "Mom, you didn't tell him about the Angels, did you?" Minutes later, Travis, whose blond hair and blue eyes matched mine, pulled me into the bathroom to ask the same question. They didn't know the Angels foretold Jerry's coming into our life and said he's the one. I'd been single six years. Getting Momma married was never far from their minds.

No, I wouldn't be telling Jerry the crystal story. Baby steps: no crystals, no Angels. Besides, if the Angels were right, I'd have plenty of time to tell him.

*

I was about to experience re-entry, a state-of-being Elisabeth clarified during the closing session. Our instructions were to "take it easy" when reuniting with family and friends. We were to avoid stress, violence, and mind-altering drugs.

I was tired. I wanted a hot shower in private, and a nap. My gentle tenant veteran, Jeff, was in Anchorage so Jerry drove me home. My duplex looked deserted in noontime light—kids at school, my tenant gone.

Because of Jeff's obsessive need for order, it felt safe to invite Jerry in for coffee. I was not disappointed: dishes put away, counters shining, clean floor, nothing out of place. I put coffee on and Jerry carried my things in from the car and brought them down to my bedroom.

As always after an absence, I took a moment to visit with my African violets that sat on a suspended shelf above the sink. Their pink and purple blooms said, "We don't bloom for just anyone. You're special," a sentiment I longed to hear from human lips. I bounced their hairy leaves to check for hydration and breathed in a coffee-scented breath of gratitude. I was glad to be home, grateful for an ordinary day.

A knock on the front door intruded. The person standing there was so unexpected it took me several seconds to recognize him as Rob, an ex-lover. I hadn't heard from him in more than a year; last I knew, he was living in Florida. I'd ended our two-year relationship after he got into a fight at the Lake Lucille Bar to defend my honor when a stranger mistook him for my son. I hadn't seen him since. His presence stumped me. After such a long absence, what was there to say?

"I was in the neighborhood." His home, before he'd moved to Florida, was south of Anchorage, a sixty-five mile drive. "Got coffee?"

I'm sure he could smell it brewing. What was there to do but ask him in? Jerry came down the hall from the bedroom as Rob reached the kitchen table. They remained standing while I introduced them, first names only. I watched them take each other's measure. Rob knew at once that I'd moved on, and, to his credit, assumed the role of family friend. Jerry appeared to regard him as an acquaintance of my eldest daughter. I served cups of steaming black coffee for all.

The men remained silent as I took my seat and lighted a cigarette. Before I'd exhaled my first lungful of smoke, the front window rattled. The flash of teeth and a nose smashed against the glass startled me. Then it was gone. My front door banged open and in walked my ex-husband Keith as if he lived there, which he never had. We'd married after the divorce from my first husband, Jesse, and he was the father of Christine and Travis, but we'd parted ways when the kids were still little. Now smiling, he strolled to the table, introduced himself to Rob and Jerry, ordered a cup of coffee as if in a restaurant, and sat down.

I hadn't moved or spoken. Even in my own home I knew my role: I made quick introductions and served him coffee.

Keith turned to Jerry. "That your Le Baron out front? I need a truck for business or I'd drive a Lincoln. More room. You workin'?"

"No."

"You workin'?" he asked of Rob.

"No. Ground's still frozen. Nothing's started yet," Rob said.

"What do you do?" Keith asked Rob, then Jerry.

"Steel worker," Rob said.

"Carpenter," Jerry said.

Not finding any connection with a steelworker, Keith turned to Jerry. "Who do you work for?" Names exchanged between the two but still no connection. I smoked, sipped coffee and watched Keith thrash about to build a platform from which he could self-promote. "Get your moose last year?"

"No, didn't hunt," Jerry said.

"This morning a cow and her calf crossed the road in front of me just past the flats." Keith made it sound as if the moose had chosen him from hundreds of other motorists to honor with their crossing. He continued to fire questions at Rob and Jerry as if from an automatic weapon—no time taken to digest answers.

I smiled into my coffee cup because I felt no urgency to direct the conversational flow. They were adults and could fend for themselves. I wasn't responsible for their feelings or actions. Only Jerry was here by invitation.

Before the workshop, I'd have been in a frenzy of embarrassment, guilt, and a need to explain. I'd have prayed for an earthquake, a moose in the yard, an armed robber to break down the door, anything to distract attention away from me and the fact that I'd been intimate with all three of these men.

Instead, I sat calmly and watched them jockey for position. What had changed? Not them. What must have changed was me, and that thought was both exciting and frightening.

After one cup of coffee, I announced I needed a shower and left the three of them at my kitchen table. Although that sounds like an exit, it was actually the opening scene of a new chapter in my life called "Truce: Men Aren't the Enemy."

CHAPTER NINE
Magic at the Fair

MORE CHANGES became apparent in the following weeks. My tyrant boss mellowed considerably and granted me the typewriter I'd asked for. As the months passed, other changes surfaced. Dead-beat Keith made his child-support payments on time, a major miracle because his attitude over the past six years toward child-support was that it was a mere suggestion on the part of the courts. Were these changes in others' behavior something I had a part in bringing about? They led me to wonder about my session on the mat. Could those few minutes have made such a significant change in me?

My interactions with men changed, become easier, and the Angels weren't taking credit. By then I'd confided a bit about the Angels to Jerry, who reacted with skepticism but didn't run from me.

Six months after the LDT, I opened my closet doors to a rainbow of color where before there had been only navy blue, black, and white. I even had a red dress. How had this happened? Without my being aware, I had replaced my drab wardrobe with clothes of many colors "like Joseph's coat in the Bible," my Appalachian mother would've said.

Even my relationship with the Angels changed some, and although it remained one of love-hate, I resisted less. Perhaps as a result, I received verification of the Angels' accuracy more often.

One such occasion happened in June, a month after the workshop. Just typing the word June makes me revisit the feelings that month produces. June in Alaska means not being tired or hungry and having lots of socializing and fun. Unfortunately, it's also a time when one is likely to make bad decisions. June's constant daylight is the culprit; it produces a mental state similar to the manic phase of bi-polar disorder.

I'd just put the kids on a plane to Arizona to spend six weeks with grandparents and was feeling good during the drive home. About fifteen miles out of Anchorage, on the right side of the highway, I saw flashes of light where none should have been. As I got closer, I saw a booth draped on three sides with black cloth. Hanging from several lines strung across tall corner poles dangled cut glass crystals, in full sun. Rainbows flashed from thousands of facets. Las Vegas couldn't have sported more glitz.

I didn't need to rush home, so I parked alongside the road. The young man behind the display of crystals looked familiar. Could this have been one of the booths at the Palmer Fair a couple of years back?

I asked to examine first one crystal, then another, but the one I wanted—a square devoid of facets that reflected colors in a way most cut-glass crystals did not—was out of my price range. For some reason, I asked the young man, "Has your life changed any since you started selling crystals?"

He responded, "Are you the Angel Lady?"

I acted as if I didn't understand, but he was not put off.

"Do you live in Wasilla? Do you write for Angels?"

I must have looked guilty because he grabbed my arm and yelled, "Amber, come here. I've found her!"

A young woman appeared to fly from the rear door of a near-by trailer. She gave the illusion

of being transported, her feet not touching the
ground from trailer to my person. I found myself
smothered by yards of musty velvet in the colors
of an ancient forest—rotted browns, mossy
greens—in the arms of a sobbing girl.

"You saved my life! I owe everything to you. I
almost killed myself. The Angels' letter saved me."

I knew exactly the letter she meant; it was one
from last year. I had rock solid memory of that
letter. The Angels had haunted me for ten days
until I'd done the thing they demanded.

This had started on the first day of the Palmer
Fair, during my opening shift in the Information
Booth for the Mat-Su Council on Alcohol and
Drug Abuse. An afternoon chill had caused
the crowds to thin. To fill the time I decided to
outline a lecture series I'd been asked to present
at the local medium-security prison. I sat down,
put pen to paper—and the Angels took control:
*This is for the lady at the crystal booth. You are
not to worry. Your children will be returned to
you after a journey across water. Once your son is
again under your roof he will begin to speak. He
is of sound mind. He is not broken. Their bodies
will profit from wholesome food and rest. The call
will come. They are safe. Worry does not help.
They know you love them. Your mother's health
will improve in your care. Give her wheat grass*

and force liquids. No red meat. The Angels love you. Angels are love.

That first day I tore the pages off the pad and made them into confetti. I was too embarrassed to do anything else. Later I tried to work on my lecture series, but, again, the minute the pen touched the page, the identical letter scribbled out. After destroying the evidence for a second time that day, I put the pad and pen away. I'd try again tomorrow.

For the next nine days, I tried to work on the lectures with the same results. It made no difference where I tried to write—at home, at the office, or sitting in the booth on the fair- grounds—the Angels wrote the same letter, word for word.

By the last day of the fair, I was frantic. The energy had shifted and now slammed my arm onto the pad with a bang; the pen became weapon-like, cutting through two, sometimes three, pages when it underlined a word. By three o'clock, when the concessionaires were packing their wares and disassembling their booths, I'd felt desperate. Not knowing what else to do, I folded the latest pages and walked to the closest booth that sold crystals.

"Can I help you?" an unkempt young man with unfocused eyes asked. His dung-colored clothes reeked of marijuana and his blonde hair was matted. I thrust the folded pages at him, did an about-face and made my escape before he could unfold the letter or ask questions.

Yes, I knew exactly which letter the young woman who was hugging me had in mind.

With her feet back on terra firma, and her composure restored, she continued, "When Jonathan read the letter you gave him, he knew it was meant for me. My ex-husband was a violent man and he'd taken my two sons and I didn't know where they were. They'd already been gone for eighteen months, and I'd given up ever finding them. My mother was very sick, but doctors couldn't find out why. She kept getting weaker and weaker. We thought sure she was dying. When we left the Palmer Fair, we drove to Seattle, so I didn't understand the part about crossing water, but something about the Angel letter felt right. I read it every day, sometimes more than once. Momma came to live with us. I changed her diet, forced liquids, gave her wheat grass, but no red meat. She got better and was able to return to work, but still no news of Bobby and Timothy.

"It was midnight, one year to the day after you gave me the letter, when I got the phone call from the police in Seward, Alaska. They'd arrested my ex. He was in jail. They told me to come get my sons. I flew up the next day over Alaska's waterways; that was the water part. Timothy, my four-year-old, didn't speak a word, but after just two months he started talking in full sentences. The Angels said he wasn't retarded so I didn't worry. Bobby, my six-year-old, slept under his bed for the longest time, but he's over that now. I get really scared when I think of where they'd be if I'd killed myself."

She added, "I have the letter in the trailer. I feel better just having it close. Do you want to see it?"

"No thanks. I remember it well."

"What can I do for you? Just name it and it's yours."

"Nothing. I've got to go." I turned towards my car, feeling suspended in time and space like in that old TV show "The Twilight Zone." If I could get to my car and drive out of there, I knew I'd be okay.

I heard the young man tell Amber, "She really liked this one." Then there were footsteps behind me and a touch on my shoulder. I had to turn around.

In his extended hand was the expensive square crystal. I tried to resist but Amber took it from him, dropped it into my purse and refused to take it back.

I placed it on my desk alongside Elisabeth's crystal to remind me: all of this really happened. It wasn't a dream. I didn't make it up.

CHAPTER TEN

The Force

WHEN ELISABETH asked me to serve as the Alaska Coordinator for Shanti Nilaya, in typical Elisabeth style she hadn't gone into detail. In my distracted state, I'd accepted without question. Two weeks later, I discovered "Alaska Coordinator" was code for "Give Jan's home phone number to any Alaska resident requesting help of any kind." I had no warning, no training, no salary.

Within a week after the LDT, I found a note on the dining table in my daughter's handwriting: "Linda—cancer patient—555-111-1234. Elisabeth said you would help."

Help how? I felt certain Elisabeth had in mind Angel writings, but I wasn't going to let that happen—ever. Although there'd been cancer patients at the workshop and up on the mat, I'd avoided personally meeting any. I'd watched other healthy, and apparently sane, participants go out of their way to spend time with the identified patients. Not me, the gal who practiced avoidance with a capital A. Her motto that week was "Never, never, never, make eye contact."

What was it about serious illness that attracted healthy people? Was it because it made them feel lucky, so they could walk away and say, "Thank God that isn't me?" Well, I didn't need to chat with terminally ill folk to be grateful I wasn't dying. With kids depending on me, I had no time for death—mine or anyone else's.

Before I returned Linda's call, I phoned Shanti Nilaya. The person who answered told me, "You'll do just fine. Elisabeth wouldn't have referred Linda to you if she wasn't confident you'd know what to do." My gut said, "They don't have a clue."

Alaska and an alcoholic ex-husband had taught me I was on my own: fail and you die. This new challenge felt no different than when I had three kids to feed, food for one day, and no money coming in for six weeks. The kids and I had survived. I reasoned that to return Linda's call couldn't be as hard as that.

I turned to the only help I knew. Okay, Angels, it's just you and me—no one else is watching. I dialed Linda's number, praying she wouldn't answer.

"Hello?"

Damn.

I introduced myself.

Linda's voice oozed palatable relief; you'd have thought I called to give her the cure she and her family longed for. She asked when we could meet, as if a visit had been promised. I put her off for a week. Anchorage was fifty miles from Wasilla. My evil-self hoped she wouldn't be able to make the trip, while my kinder side experienced a tinge of guilt. I felt grateful that the Angels were quiet on the subject.

The day before our appointment, Patty, Linda's friend, called. Linda was having a bad week and wouldn't be able to travel; could I possibly come to her? I wanted to say no, that I had obligations I couldn't cancel. But I didn't. I took down directions and said I'd be there tomorrow.

I didn't sleep well that night, but by morning I'd contrived a plan based on one of Elisabeth's lectures: I'd listen. Isn't that what she'd said all patients wanted—to be heard? Mouth shut. Ears open. I'd listen. As a preventive measure against interfering Angels, I rid myself of pens and paper.

None in my pockets, none in my purse.

On the hour drive to Anchorage I had plenty of time to sort my feelings. I discovered it wasn't Linda that frightened me. It was meeting Linda-the-host-to-Death that caused my hands to tremble and my stomach to clench.

I remembered the first time I'd considered death as a reality: it had been when I looked into the red, wrinkled face of my first-born child. The baby in my arms was evidence of new life, therefore the opposite must also be true: death too was real. Postpartum depression? Perhaps. For instead of joy and celebration of life, my baby girl's birth had pressed death into my conscious mind. My next thought was that my parents would die, and there was nothing I could do to prevent it.

That evening Jesse returned home to find his wife in her nightclothes, sitting where he had left me hours before, holding our sleeping daughter, and sobbing. That remembered feeling of helplessness swept over me again as I drove toward Anchorage. Tears blurred the road. I blinked them away, opened the car window a crack before lighting up. Nicotine always helped.

I found Linda's house, parked a little way down the block, turned off the motor, sat in the car and smoked another cigarette—one last fix before entering a non-smoking zone. Nothing outside the car window screamed a-woman-is-dying-right-over-there. It was just an ordinary neighborhood, an ordinary house, an ordinary day. I had a second cigarette, dropped the butt in the street, shook my shoulders and prepared myself for a dreadful experience.

I'd seen the faces of new life with the births of my three children; now I would see the face of death in Linda's. Those were my thoughts when Patty invited me into the living room and indicated I should sit on the sofa across from a recliner covered with a flannel sheet. Clutter buried the chair-side table: water, lip balm, prescription bottles, wadded tissues, remote control, flashlight. An open book lay face down beside a child's drawing of a rainbow and hearts. All was evidence of long-term illness.

Patty brought me coffee and explained that Linda's husband was at work and her children at school, and Linda had just gone to the bathroom. The drapes were drawn. I felt cold.

Linda came into the room dragging an oxygen tank on a wheeled cart. I averted my eyes, embarrassed. It took several minutes and help from Patty for Linda to be seated and arranged. I sipped my coffee and wished for a smoke.

"Thank you for coming," Linda said.

I set my mug down, stretched on a smile, prepared for the worst and looked up.

Time stopped.

No. It didn't stop; it bridged a moment from twenty years past into the present. Shining on Linda's face, where I had expected to see death, I saw instead a presence I'd met once before. I recognized it. It recognized me. Yet I had no name for it. I watched Linda's face as the light—though it wasn't exactly a light—winked and laughed at me. It made me angry. I wanted to scream and run.

I don't remember much of that visit except that it was short and I was surprised when, on my way out, Patty asked me to come back next week. "You've really been a help. Linda is resting more peacefully."

I was astounded. I had already concluded that the visit must have been a disappointment for Linda. I certainly hadn't helped. I could barely pretend to listen as she talked about losing her life, losing her children, losing her husband, losing her faith. She said Elisabeth had hinted that perhaps I could help her.

I didn't even wait to get to my car before lighting up; my hands shook so much I cupped the lighter with both hands. I drove to a nearby church and parked out of sight of the street in the empty parking lot and turned off the motor. Elisabeth's voice rattled in my head, "The natural expression of fear is the scream, a deep belly scream." I made sure no one was around, and— though I hadn't been able to do it at the LDT—I filled my lungs and screamed and screamed and screamed. Then I cried and remembered.

*

I'd been only nineteen, married one year to Jesse, my high school sweetheart. Guilt welled up in me each time memory brought him back to life—twelve years dead now, drowned while scuba diving near Santa Cruz in the California ocean. I'd managed to save him once from drowning, but when he was in such danger again, I wasn't there, and even if I were, could I have changed anything?

The beach where he drowned wasn't the one where I first met that... that... something I'd seen in Linda's face. No, that had happened off the Coronado beach the day of the San Diego yacht races. Jesse had decided to swim out to the racing spar, a buoy used to mark the race course. I didn't want to but joined him anyway.

Jesse

After we swam beyond the breakers, beyond the sound of surf and out of sight of the beach, we stopped so I could rest. Jesse treaded water while I flipped onto my back to get my second wind. Within minutes, I felt strength flow back into my limbs. But Jesse's thin physique meant he had a negative ratio of body fat to muscle, so he couldn't float. He couldn't rest.

The racing spar didn't appear any closer than when we'd left the beach. What should we do? Continue to the spar or turn back? Jesse's fatigue argued for the closest solution. We reasoned that the spar had to be closer and surely he could rest once we reached it. It seemed we stopped for hours, but it couldn't have been. We reached the spar but discovered there were no handholds, no platform; it was just a pole anchored somehow so that it rolled and bobbed about. The circumference was such that Jesse couldn't reach around it to pull himself out of the water. He could only wrap his arms around it for support.

My husband began to shiver and cramp. As I floated, and he treaded water weakly, we discussed our options. He didn't have the strength to swim back to the beach. There was no rescue in sight. I could rest by floating. It was decided: I would swim to the beach and send help. He promised to hang on no matter what. My fear as I turned toward the beach was that I would be too long in gaining land and Jesse would give up, turn loose of the spar and drown. I could see the next day's headlines: "Widowed at Nineteen!" I swam harder.

Jesse and the spar were soon out of sight leaving me bobbing in its departing waves. With nothing to give me perspective, I lost the sensation of moving forward. A change in light caused me to glance over my right shoulder. A teal-green wall blocked the sky from my view. It was almost on top of me. Then I heard the motor and understood: the wall was a ship's hull, and I was about to be drawn beneath it. Fear that I'd be chewed up and spit back into the ocean as fish chum fueled a burst of speed. The hull continued to gain on me until the wall became an overhang, the bow visible overhead. I knew I was lost.

Then just at that moment, and for no apparent reason, the motor shut down. The ship stopped. I was able to put distance between myself and sure death. When I rolled onto my back to catch my breath, the boat turned and was soon out of sight, leaving me bobbing in its departing waves. Again I was alone on the ocean surface.

When I started to swim again, I became disoriented. I wasn't sure if I was swimming toward the beach or away. Time and direction were both lost due to my fatigue and the flat light of the overcast day. I felt as if I were on top of a mountain of water. Was I swimming parallel to the beach, or away from it and out to sea? Had Jesse given up and let go of the spar? Was he already dead?

In my exhausted state of mind, I was positive I was now swimming parallel to the beach. I believed I was too far out ever to gain shore. I felt certain Jesse was dead. I was his wife, I would know. I was too tired to continue. I didn't want to continue. Nothing was worth the effort. I stopped swimming.

But my arms kept moving. My legs kept kicking, even after I told them to quit. "Stop! Damn it, stop! Please stop!" My arms and legs kept moving. I was no longer in control of my body. I swam in spite of my desire to stop, my command to stop. Something from out of nowhere, A Force, controlled my limbs. I couldn't stop them. By then, I was pissed. I was ready to accept dying of exhaustion and drowning, and this Force just took over whether I wanted it or not.

We both survived that day, but later Jesse and I divorced. Eventually, he returned to the ocean, to Santa Cruz, where he died.

*

Twenty three years later, I saw, dancing on Linda's face, that same something. It had laughed at me! I'd met that Force again, the one that propelled my arms and legs against my will. Wouldn't you think I'd be grateful? After all, that Force, that energy, that something, had kept me alive, had sent help for Jesse. I wasn't grateful. I was frightened. I never spoke of how I made it to the beach back then. I'd told no one, not even Jesse. I wiped it from memory until today.

Why was I frightened? It was daylight. I was inside a locked car in a church parking lot. No rabid dogs circled the car, no criminals threatened to break my windows. I wasn't being held at gunpoint. I was safe. I considered myself rational. I preferred the scientific to the supernatural, Angels notwithstanding. What happened in Linda's living room? Why was I frightened?

This marked the second time I'd met a Force, an Energy, that existed outside of personality—a Force that had no regard for the wishes of the person who housed it. The Force, that I considered the power of Being and Living, was totally selfish, was concerned only for its own survival. In my case, you could argue that it knew best. I was alive because of it. Three beautiful children lived because I lived.

As important as that memory seemed, I still needed to determine what was best for Linda. I did remember enough of our visit to know she was ready to be through with the pain, through with the tests and the treatments. She was going to die; it was just a matter of when. In Linda's case, who or what was the Force serving?

Sitting in that church parking lot, I knew this power had nothing to do with Jesus or the Father or the Holy Ghost. I didn't know what it meant, but I did know I'd moved beyond the doctrine that my Pentecostal minister father taught. I'd touched something that didn't fit between the leather bindings of my grandmother's Bible.

And I was frightened.

CHAPTER ELEVEN

Toilet Paper

AS THE SUN SHONE later and later into Alaska's summer nights, I struggled to pull myself together after visiting Linda. When I felt on level ground again, I called Shanti Nilaya to ask Sheila what, exactly, were the duties of a coordinator. When I identified myself, she said, "Linda called to thank Elisabeth for her referral. She thinks you're wonderful. Didn't I tell you not to worry?"

I was speechless. Me? Wonderful? How could that be? I remembered nothing of our conversation; I could barely remember Linda herself, so preoccupied was I with my own discomfort and the light that shone from her face.

Deserving or not, I drank in Sheila's praise as if it were sweet wine.

"All of us here, especially Elisabeth, are excited that you're our contact in Alaska." What Sheila said next caused me to forget any questions I'd meant to ask. "Elisabeth wants to know when to expect some 'yellow pages.' Said you'd know what she meant. And I was to remind you to write 'personal' on the envelope."

I knew precisely what she meant. Elisabeth wanted me to ask the Angels if they had anything for her. I was to mail any resulting pages to the Escondido office and Sheila would forward them to Elisabeth, wherever on the globe she might be. Resistance welled up in me and dread replaced my high spirits.

In my experience to date, Angels seldom wrote for absent people. When they did, it was at the Angels' own insistence, like at the state fair when they wrote for the woman with the missing sons.

I didn't want to write for an absentee Elisabeth, especially when my deeper concern was that Elisabeth had broken my first rule about Angel writings: take the writings as a third opinion, consider what they say, but don't make important decisions based solely on them. Yet she'd apparently taken their advice to get a financial manager, since she announced the next day at the

LDT that she was seeking a bookkeeper. What if the Angels wrote something else and Elisabeth acted on it immediately, and then it proved harmful in some way?

Yet, it did seem that some power outside of reason had been at work in the odd events that took place at the workshop. What about when Elisabeth, without an introduction, asked me to take her on a tour? Me. She chose me, when there were a hundred others she might have asked. Before she was even seated in the car, she asked about my spirit guides, which in turn opened the subject of the Angels.

Even more perplexing, how was I to account for the moose-horn ring incident? The identical crystals we'd exchanged? One fact I could not deny was that if the Angels hadn't written for Elisabeth that day in her cabin, I probably wouldn't be the Alaska Coordinator.

All is as it should be, the Angels whispered into my ear as I hung up the phone.

That evening in the twilight space before sleep, I remembered Sheila's voice, her calm assured tone. The other staff members came to mind. How comfortable they'd seemed at the workshop no matter what was happening on the mat. The stories of abuse, illness or death that participants screamed out seemed not to touch the staff; they remained outside that pain, not distant from the person on the mat, but outside the pain. I wanted to learn their secret.

To do that, my only hope was to remain the Alaska Coordinator.

*

By September—when Christine and Travis returned from their summer visit with grandparents—the phone calls from cancer patients, their family members and friends, had multiplied. Many nights I fixed dinner with the phone tucked between ear and shoulder while strangers asked for help I still felt unprepared to give. What did I know of terminal cancer? What did I know of surviving a son's suicide? I was the Alaska Coordinator. I was supposed to know.

Therefore, I listened and repeated phrases Elisabeth had used: What could you have done differently? You miss him/her terribly. Who wasn't there for you? Where were you when you got the call? Phrases that made me cringe when I'd first heard them. They sounded so cruel; I was shocked at the relief they seemed to bring. I poured these phrases into the phone and listened to strangers tell me of secret hatreds, confide their

Leota and her kids, Janet, Christine and Travis

guilt, their longing for absent loves. Confusion and feelings of inadequacy haunted me awake and asleep. I needed to know more, needed to know what Sheila and the others knew.

October came. Gone were the long days of summer daylight; and gone was my eldest daughter, Janet, nineteen, now living in New York City with her fiancé. Since my divorce from Keith, Janet had been my help-mate. We'd shared the workload of family, and I missed her.

Soon, the darkness of Alaska's winter stole my energy and can-do attitude. At work I was assigned additional duties and had to work sometimes three nights a week. Christine and Travis learned to use the microwave and cooked for themselves more than I liked.

Despite the darkness, constant fatigue, and hassles with work and family, I clung to my role of Coordinator. Besides fielding phone calls, Sheila asked me to form a support group for LDT workshop alumni. According to her, these duties included locating a space, setting a time, and attending as a peer. Since Art and I were the only locals I knew who had attended the LDT, I didn't believe a Wasilla area Shanti Nilaya Support Group was possible. Still, I told a few people and posted a notice on the grocery store bulletin board. I prepared for no-shows.

To my surprise, despite heavy snow and temperatures in the teens, my living room filled to overflowing. Among the crowd were my first patient, Linda, with her friend Patty, who drove up from Anchorage along with two friends. Linda, though thin, looked almost healthy in her pastel sweater, wool slacks, and flowing blonde wig. Her improved appearance served as my initiation into the ups and downs of cancer treatment. Though she looked good, she was still dying.

After introductions, Linda held the group spellbound; no one so much as shifted in their seats as she shared how, at thirty-seven-years, her life was being cut short. Due to lack of tissues, I had to distribute rolls of toilet paper as Linda talked about her losses. "My children are losing their mother, my husband his wife. But they don't understand: I'm losing everyone. I'll have no high school graduations, no weddings, no grandchildren. I'm losing it all."

Someone sniffed, but Linda didn't look up and her voice hardened. "Last week my husband yelled at me because I fired our housekeeper. I walked in and found her ironing my husband's white shirt. I lost it. I fired her on the spot and then went to bed and cried all afternoon." Her foot kicked out and a roll of toilet paper spun across the floor. "He didn't understand how important ironing his shirts was to me. It was the last job I could still do for my family."

Someone asked, "Linda, what is the one thing you want us to know?"

"That no life is a waste. Every life is a lifetime. Some are just longer than others."

The thoughtful silence that filled the room was broken by a young woman sitting on the floor. "What do you mean?"

Linda spoke directly to her. "When I hear someone say, 'what a waste, so-and-so was only seven, or sixteen, or thirty- eight when they died,' I want to scratch their eyes out. Don't they see that for the person who died, that was their whole life? I don't want anyone to say my life was a waste. No life is a waste. Some lives are just longer than others."

No one found much to say after that, and the meeting closed. Some members exchanged phone numbers and asked when we'd meet again. That caught me by surprise since I hadn't expected anyone to show up this time. Three home-health workers stayed late and asked about training. Could I speak to their peers about the terminally ill patients they had on their caseloads?

Terror seized me. Now I was sure to be found out for the phony I believed myself to be. I promised to call after I checked my calendar. That promise made me a liar; I had no plans.

Acid poured into my stomach as I reviewed the day's events. Any fool could see I was buried under an avalanche of misinformation, and it was all my own doing. The people who'd attended today's meeting had expectations of an ongoing support group led by a knowledgeable person. That was not me.

Call Sheila, we'll handle the rest.

Yeah, just call Sheila and tell her I'm an idiot. How do you think you'll handle that?

Call.

I didn't call Sheila.

I loaded the dishwasher, straightened the living room and stewed.

Travis appeared and asked, "When's dinner? I'm hungry."

*

By mid-December of '82, with less than five hours of daylight, and temperatures in the single digits, I hit bottom. All I wanted to do was sleep and eat. Nothing helped: not the winter solstice when we started to gain daylight minutes, not even the arrival of Momma's Christmas box from Arizona.

The Christmas box was always full of individually wrapped presents, some to be opened immediately, others to wonder about until Christmas morning. In a sense, the little packages were all gifts to me, a single mom who, especially at Christmas time, had to make every dollar do double duty.

Momma's box did more than increase Christmas bounty. It sprinkled excitement. Each small package was an unknown, a brightly wrapped possibility. But the best gift was always the one with my name on it, the one not paid for from my budget, the only gift that surprised me each year.

Pretty much everything else in my life held worry and conflict.

Janet called from New York at least once a week with stories of drunken partying that should have frightened her; they sure scared me. What was I, an alcoholism counselor, to do about that? I was sure my daughter Christine, now ten, was experimenting with pot.

Heck, I was experimenting with pot. What would my boss say if that ever became general knowledge? Since the Ravin v. Alaska ruling in 1975, marijuana was legal, so I wasn't breaking the law, but still.

The boss knew I acted in the community theater, but I was sure he didn't know about the pot smoking and boozing at cast parties. Recovering alcoholics like him thought anyone who drank or smoked pot was an addict. The Council's official stand was that some people can drink/smoke all their lives and never become addicted (which I hoped included Janet), but my boss didn't believe that was possible.

I felt like a depressed circus juggler, except that if I dropped a ball my whole life would shatter.

*

One conflict I had was about The Group, teenage and young adult devotees of the Angels. These friends of Janet's had been coming to our home regularly since before she moved to New York, and they still appeared at the house at least once a week, hoping to catch me writing notes from the Angels. Janet herself scorned the whole subject of Angels and the writings, but her friends wanted to gather around in my kitchen, asking questions and delighting in the answers.

These were not your go-to-church-every-Sunday kids; they lived on the fringe—school drop-outs, some on probation. One boy liked to blow up things and didn't have an address.

Taken together, though, they were thoughtful, questioning young people who argued about the true meaning of the Angels' lessons. They devised experiments to test the Angels' theories. After a lesson on Loving With Intent, a law of nature, according to the Angels, The Group made a pact: the next time they found themselves in an argument, they'd visualize sending pink arrows inscribed with the word love into the eyes of the person they were in conflict with. They chose pink because the Angels said it was the color of love energy.

Each promised to observe the results and report back. What the heck, I thought, it can't hurt, and at least they won't be using real weapons. It was their questioning attitude that kept me writing for them. Members of The Group didn't swallow the writings whole, unlike some adults I'd written for—Elisabeth, to name one.

I had another reason to continue writing for The Group. Each kid made positive changes in his or her life based on the Angel lessons.

Writing for them in private was one thing. But I worried how my boss would perceive me if the writings became a subject of gossip in town. Would my job be at risk? In my last job I'd been verbally assaulted by a minister who stormed into my office and accused me of being a witch. The parents of Troy, a Group member, had sent the minister to berate me.

A couple of weeks later I'd earned an apology from that preacher.

My phone rang on a bright Sunday morning. It was Troy, begging me to pick him up from jail. His parents were out of town and the police were releasing him. When I arrived, I found him barefooted and shirtless. He'd been rousted from bed and not given time to dress. Once in the car, he told me he'd been arrested for breaking into homes and stealing stereos.

"Did you do it?" I asked.

"You know I did."

"What makes you think I know?"

That's when he dug folded pages of Angel writings from his jeans pocket. No shoes, no shirt, but he had Angel writings in his pocket. Sometimes when the Angels wrote messages for others through me, I'd just read the name it was intended for and hand it over, so I didn't know what his pages said. We'd all looked at Troy that night and expected him to explain, but he said nothing, just folded his pages, finished his cigarette, and left. None of us knew that he'd been stealing.

Now, he read that message from two weeks earlier. The Angels had chewed him out: *Troy you are cause of energy imbalance. Make this right. You know whence we speak.* They'd dictated a lesson about money and property as symbols of energy spent and the law of balance. *Man works. Receives* *dollars. Dollars are symbol of energy spent. Man gives dollars to farmer for energy used to grow corn. Energy balanced. Universe demands balance. You have caused an imbalance. <u>Make this right.</u>* The words "make this right" had been underlined with such force it cut through the paper, the Angels' way of reinforcing a point—screaming, you might say.

The outcome was positive; Troy was put on probation, mended his ways, and made restitution. His parents were delighted, and the minister who'd called me a witch left brusque words of apology on my voice mail. At the next writing, the Angels thanked him for his contribution to universal balance.

How could I not write for this group?

9/2/79

Jan you are to use the typewritter from now on. we like it better than the pen a
and it doesn't use so much paper. The lesson tonight is on loveing with power
yes love again we told you that this would be mentioned often as it is the first
law of creation. love with intent is the way to build a world that was built
beofre. the world before was not of this plane but of your plane. we speak
of a physical world not a spirtual world. The world before was called a garden in
the bible. And a garden it was, where the plants, animals and world grew as
if enchanted. But the truth was all loved all and the all way whole. The love
was the secret. In those days the angels were one with man and man was one
with the animals and the plants of the earth and with the earth also. It will
be this way again when man learns to love with intent. The angels are to help
man learn to love with intent. Loving with intent is to create and to love

A page of Leota's angel writings.

CHAPTER TWELVE
Phone Terrors

CALLS FROM the terminally ill and their families increased. I continued to feed them phrases I'd heard Elisabeth say. With repetition it got easier to say things like, "How do you feel about that?"

However, the details of their stories weighed me down. I had no easy answers for the weeping mother of the toddler with leukemia, or for the angry woman whose husband abandoned her when their child's murder went unsolved for six months. I felt I had nothing to offer these people. No solutions. No hope.

Too many evenings after Christine and Travis retreated to their bedrooms, I'd be at the kitchen table, phone balanced on my shoulder, listening to one sad story after another. I listened and smoked cigarette after cigarette. I repeated meaningless phrases to anonymous callers and gathered their sadness into me.

The telephone became the spring from which all misery flowed. By March, I resembled one of Pavlov's dogs: the phone rang, my stomach clenched. I knew each caller would be another desperate person asking "What should I do?" I didn't know what I should do, let alone what they should do.

The monthly support group continued to meet, community awareness spread, attendance increased. Home-health workers attended regularly and even brought boxes of tissues to replace my rolls of toilet paper. Cancer patients called and asked to share their experience and insights with us.

At the January meeting, Otto, a tall, extremely thin, victim of lung cancer, told us in his raspy, breathless voice of his daughter's unreasonable anger. He lived alone in a remote cabin; a wood stove was his only heat. She wanted him in her home where she could care for him more easily. They fought. He'd locked his doors and refused to answer her calls. "My life. I'll decide." Coughing and choking cut off his rant.

Those seated near him looked sorrowful and offered him tissues, but he batted their hands away and drew a handkerchief from his pant's pocket. I wanted to kick the chair from under the selfish old coot.

In February his daughter called. She'd found him dead, frozen in his bed. She'd had to call the police to gain entrance. I had no comforting words for her. "I'm sorry for your loss" felt empty.

All these people who phoned, and those who attended the monthly support groups, looked to me as if I were someone especially knowledgeable about death, dying, and bereavement. I'd read Elisabeth's books, and been to one LDT conference, but what did I know about therapy in this area?

I felt like a terrible fraud. How could the Shanti Nilaya staff imagine I had the skills to help the dying and grieving people they kept referring to me? The only counseling training I'd ever had was through the trade school, ANTI, which focused solely on alcoholism, and I considered that education a joke. It had been an exercise I waltzed through the previous year to gain a certificate. The idea was that it would grandfather me in as an addictions counselor if, or when, licensure became a requirement in Alaska.

The mission of ANTI was to teach native Alaskans to intervene with their own alcoholic community members, on-site in native villages. As a blue-eyed blonde woman, I'd been an interloper, and I became aware that I lived an unearned privileged life because of my Scotch-Irish great-grandparents.

I held no illusions that I'd actually earned those twenty-four college credits, half in psychology, half in sociology. Certainly, I hadn't learned how to counsel these new kinds of clients. For that I still relied on Angel whispers, Elisabeth's phrases, and my experience living the Twelve Steps of AA/Al-Anon.

Did I decline my certificate? Of course not, but I accepted it feeling unprepared.

And now, with no therapy qualifications except that irrelevant training from ANTI, I was counseling dying people.

*

All that winter, as referrals increased and my frustration deepened, the Angels insisted I call Sheila to ask about therapy training for myself. I didn't heed their urgings. I knew training in Elisabeth's style of therapy—which she called "externalization" or "mat-work" (but an article I'd read called "a combination of Gestalt and primal scream")—cost money. Money I didn't have.

At every writing session, though, the Angels started and ended with: *Call Sheila, we'll handle the details.* By the end of March, they'd worn me down.

Sheila responded with what sounded like a script: "All trainees are required to have attended at least one LDT before they can apply to be trained. Then they must attend three intensive training seminars and co-facilitate at one LDT with Elisabeth. The training seminars are three-hundred fifty dollars each and last three days, Friday thru Sunday. Are you interested?"

"I'm interested but I don't have the airfare, let alone seminar fees. Plus, I can't leave my job and the kids that long."

"Why not organize training in Alaska? Then you could attend for free. Elisabeth has said we need to host a training seminar in the northwest. Can't get more northwest than Alaska, can we?"

"How would I do that?"

"You reserve the lodge, hire cooks and kitchen staff, and get ten volunteer participants willing to let the facilitators-in-training work with them on the mat. I'll send you the materials you need, pay all expenses, announce the seminar in the newsletter and arrange for the trainers. Probably Carol and Nancy; they have free time in August."

I was elated until I hung up the phone. Then doubt seized me. Where was I to find people who knew about Elisabeth's externalization process, let alone anyone who wanted to be trained in it? Who, with full knowledge of what was expected of them, would volunteer to get on a mat and scream out secret pain?

Impossible! If I'd known I was expected to beat on a phone book in front of strangers, let alone cry until I vomited, I'd never have attended my first LDT.

Schedule a date, we'll fill the slots. I hated it when the Angels jumped in unannounced -and made promises I was convinced they couldn't keep—promises that put my reputation as a sane addictions counselor at risk.

*

Meier Lake Lodge, that ugly red-brown building that embarrassed its beautiful pine forest, lake and mountain setting, didn't look much different than it had the year before when I first met Elisabeth. The green, glacier-topped mountains and ice-free lake testified to a different season now and reminded me of all that had transpired since I was last here. Back then I'd come in ignorance of Elisabeth's work with cancer patients and others facing life's final transition. Now I came to unburden myself of the pain and suffering I'd absorbed from listening to the dying and bereaved and to learn how better to help them.

Instead of one hundred-plus participants like the first time, now there were only twelve. We had no need of the small log cabins scattered along the wooden pathways under the pines. We, the trainers and the trainees, were housed in the building adjacent to the ugly lodge that bore the sign Staff's Quarters.

Same as the last time, eating and socializing happened on the lodge's top floor. The workroom was down a flight of stairs. The same back-breaking, butt-assaulting folding chairs were arranged in a semi-circle facing the stage. Same song pamphlets on every seat, their pages curling, their spines stapled in the centers. Same view from the north glass walls overlooking the lake.

Carol, a large woman from California with a baritone voice, opened her lecture with, "It's not possible to feel another's pain."

I'd accepted that theory from Elisabeth at the LDT, but now I wanted to shout, "Liar!" I was here because the constriction in my chest, caused by the sobs of the mother whose child was murdered, had become unbearable. I wanted to stop the nightmares of my own children being murdered.

Don't tell me I didn't feel the pain of those anonymous callers, I argued silently. I didn't see their faces, but I felt their pain. For months, my stomach had been so knotted I had to skip lunch. Not only did worry over the calls I handled at home in the evenings stay with me, but all day at work I handled problems like women with black eyes and drunken husbands at home who'd say they'd run into a door in the dark. How dare Carol say I didn't feel the pain of others?

"The only pain you feel is your own," she continued. "Another's story pushes on your repressed pain and is misidentified as feeling the other's pain. When in pain, physical or emotional, one cannot be fully present; therefore, to help others you must empty your own reservoir of repressed pain. In Elisabeth's words, 'Complete your unfinished business.' That's why we are here this weekend, to start that process."

"How do I know what my unfinished business is?" a trainee from Anchorage asked. I wanted to kiss her.

"You'll know by Saturday," Carol said. Her words felt like a slap in the face. I decided I didn't like Carol as she moved into explaining Elisabeth's theory of the Four Quadrants. "Simply put," she lectured, "each individual is comprised of four quadrants: physical, emotional, intellectual, and spiritual. These quadrants mature at different ages. When they work in harmony, you have a balanced, healthy individual."

Four Quadrants sounded reasonable. I learned later that they were drawn from Jungian Psychology, but to me they were similar to the AA practice of self-inventory, a principle I valued and taught at the Council. Inventory served as a tool to help newly sober individuals maintain balance while putting their fractured lives back together: They needed to eat well, get exercise, and sleep (the physical quadrant); maintain control of emotions, especially resentments (emotional quadrant); do daily reading to challenge the mind and be informed (intellectual quadrant); and connect with a Higher Power as the source of serenity (spiritual quadrant).

Though I could accept the Four Quadrants theory, I refused to budge on the issue of feeling the pain of others. I prided myself on forging connections with clients through shared painful experiences. They knew I felt for them, with them; they saw it on my face, they heard it in my voice.

After the morning break, Nancy, the facilitator from Vermont, delivered the last lecture. Hers was on the Five Emotions, their survival purpose and natural and unnatural expression. She named them: anger, fear, grief, jealousy, and love.

The survival purpose of anger, she began, was not, as I'd supposed, to protect us. According to Nancy, it was to cause change in our lives. "Nothing ever changes unless someone gets royally pissed," she said. The natural expression of anger was easy—hitting, yelling, what I'd seen happen during mat work.

But, when Nancy said the unnatural expression of anger was cancer, ulcers, and heart disease, I choked. Did she mean all we had to do to cure these illnesses was to rid ourselves of unfinished business? Was that why Elisabeth, a medical doctor, believed she could smoke safely? Because she had no repressed anger?

I breathed that idea deep into my nicotine-stained lungs. As long as I emptied my reservoir of repressed anger, I could continue to inhale a pack a day and not worry about lung cancer. This unfinished business sounded like very powerful stuff.

Nancy continued, "All fears except those of falling and loud noises are unnatural ones you've learned." She repeated what I'd learned at the LDT conference: The natural expression of fear was the scream. I remembered Elizabeth saying that hospitals should have screaming rooms for the parents of seriously ill or dying children "to scream away their fear."

Yet I remained foggy on the benefit of screaming, mostly because when Elisabeth had prompted me to scream at the LDT, I couldn't. My throat had closed and nothing came out but a squeak. I'd hit the phone books, and my throat had opened enough to let me talk, but the words that emerged were spoken, not screamed.

On the other hand, I'd loosened up and screamed in my parked car after meeting Linda the first time. Had it relieved my pain and fear? Perhaps, but it hadn't relieved me of feeling unskilled and terrified when I dealt with people who were dying or in anguish. Did that unfinished business mean I was destined to experience ulcers and become the victim of an anxiety disorder? When Nancy said grief was our tool to deal with losses large and small, and that tears were the natural expression of grief, I smiled. At least I got that one right. Heaven knew that in my lifetime I'd cried buckets. Even listening to these lectures made me cry.

When she said, "Tears are inappropriate for expressing anger," I was dumbstruck. I always cried when angry. Couldn't I get anything right?

Jealousy, she said, was our natural motivator, and she used "little sister wants to ride a two-wheeler like big brother" as an example. Little sister would work extra hard to achieve the skills she needed to copy her brother.

I could accept this but saw it more as a play on words than anything I could use with my clients. Hate, envy, and passive-aggressive behavior were the result, she said, of repressed jealousy. At least there were no fatal diseases in that list.

It was Nancy's explanation of love that triggered a flood of bile to my stomach. Yes, babies died due to failure-to-thrive, lack of nurturing, lack of love, as she called it. Her assertion that parents taught their children "prostitution" as the means to obtain love, infuriated me; my face got hot and tears strung my eyes. I'd done no such thing.

"Our actions more than words teach this," she said. "Get good grades and I'll love you. Do as I say and I'll love you." This she called prostitution? My chest felt tight, like I would burst if I didn't get out of the room. I needed a cigarette.

When we returned from break, we found our chairs folded up against the wall and five mattresses scattered about on the floor. We had no choice but to stand. "Who wants to start?" Carol asked us six trainees. Without hesitation, a frail, tanned young man walked to the mat next to Carol and sat down. Carol addressed the rest of us. "As feelings come up for you, take your place on a mat and someone will join you as the facilitator. Nancy and I will monitor your process."

What she didn't say would have filled a text book. I wished I had one—anything to tell me what to do, what to expect. Were half of us going to assume the roles of facilitators with no further instructions?

The young man took the hose into his slender hands and twisted it. I felt embarrassed for him and wanted Carol to say something to put him at ease. Was I, as Carol's lecture suggested, to believe it was my own embarrassment I felt? Did I want Carol to put me at ease? Maybe. All I knew was that I wanted the silence to end.

"It's not fair!" Smack! came from the young man on the mat, and I exhaled, finally.

Almost immediately, while the young man continued his mat work, a silver-haired woman walked to a mat near the back wall and sat on it. She was joined by another trainee who took the squatting position of a facilitator at the mat's edge. They whispered. The older woman shook her head, then picked up the hose and gave the phone book a gentle tap.

My eyes drew back to Carol at the front of the room, but she appeared unaware of anyone other than the man on her mat who was now holding a pillow and sobbing into it. Two others walked to mats and assumed client/facilitator positions.

Helen, the fellow trainee at my elbow, gave me a nudge and indicated a mat with a head tilt. I raced her to the mat and squatted by its side, which made her the client and me the facilitator. Now what?

Helen grabbed the hose, yelled "son-of-a-bitch," and hit the phone book with a resounding whack. Her quick movements startled me but I was also relieved. Evidently, she knew what to do, and my only duty was to restack the phone books within striking range without being hit. By my side were other tools—tissues, a bath towel, and a pillow. I'd seen Elisabeth employ these at the LDT to facilitate different emotions, but what was I to do with them?

Soon my client wore herself out attacking an absent abusive father, and moved into tears. I handed her tissues. Through her sobs, she asked her long-dead mother, "Why? Why didn't you stop him? Why did you stay?"

I could barely hear her through the noise in the room. Five other facilitators-in-training, in the roles of clients, were screaming, whacking, crying, or talking. I found it impossible to focus. My insides were trembling. Each whack felt like an attack. Why had I thought I wanted to learn this?

Without any help from me, Helen stopped crying, climbed off the mat and stood over me with fists on hips. My turn now.

CHAPTER THIRTEEN

Death by Towel

I CRAWLED onto the mattress.

I removed my shoes and placed them side-by-side on the floor. Helen knelt in the facilitator's position. Neither of us spoke as I moved to the mat's center and remained on all fours, feeling the stretch in my lower back. "Shall we start?" Helen asked.

A tear splashed onto my hand. "I don't know where to begin."

Nancy joined us. "Why the tears?"

I rocked back onto my heels. "I don't know. Angry maybe. But I don't want to hit anything."

"What are you angry about?"

"Don't know. . . (Long pause.) . . . At men who hit women."

"Pick up the hose, grip it in both hands and raise it above your head. Bring it straight down."

I'd already done this at the LDT; I'd said angry words, beaten phone books, and humiliated myself by throwing up in public. I hadn't screamed, though. True, I'd felt good the next day but I still didn't want to unleash those feelings again. Wasn't once enough?

"I don't want to hit anything."

"I know. Just give it a try."

"Hitting is wrong. I don't want to hit anything."

Nancy handed me several tissues. "Who hit you?"

I blew my nose. "My ex, but he was drunk. He didn't mean it." Did I really say that? I knew better, but it seemed my emotions still believed otherwise.

She laid the dark red hose across my knees. "Put your anger out here where it won't hurt anyone." She slapped the stack of books with the flat of her hand.

"I don't feel angry." Yet I wondered why I was resisting so much. Were the things inside me so awful that I was terrified to unleash them?

"Just try. See what comes up." And she smacked the books again.

I picked up the hose and tapped the mat.

"Over your head and down."

"I can't."

"Just give it a try." Her voice developed an edge. "Now."

I raised the hose. Bam.

"Again."

Bam.

"Again."

No more encouragement was needed. I put my weight into the blows. It felt great. I recalled fifth grade when I'd bloodied the nose of the fat girl with corkscrew hair and glasses who called me chicken. I'd felt such relief. The striking hose rained with such force I was lifted off my heels. Then Nancy insisted I use words. "Anything. Make a sound."

"Stop!" That one spoken word broke the dam. My tears dried and my voice burst forth. "Stop, you no-good son of a bitch! Shit. Fuck. Son-of-a-bitch. Son-of-a-bitch. Son-of-a-bitch!"

A surge of energy welled up from the base of my spine: hot, swirling, explosive. It transported me back seven years. I wasn't remembering. I was there again, in the moment just before his fist slammed into my face. "Don't you dare!" I screamed. "Coward. Pick on someone your own size." The words I'd wanted to shriek at my ex—

but had not for fear of being hit—spewed into the room, punctuated by bam, bam, bam.

How much time passed? I have no memory. Yet in the turn of a moment, I felt bored with my ex, bored with hitting. I flipped the hose into the debris of torn pages and broken-backed books. Except for my stiff legs, I felt energized and clear-headed.

Helen took my right hand and held it gently in hers. We gazed at my skinned knuckles. I must have missed with the hose and caught a book's sharp edge with my bare fists, but I'd felt no pain. Helen rummaged through the trash by the mat, found band-aids and bandaged my wounds. "It wasn't my fault. I did nothing wrong," I said to the top of her head.

She looked into my eyes and smiled. "Gal, you're a real tiger. Remind me to never make you angry."

"I don't know what happened. I never get angry."

In her soft Texas drawl she said, "Maybe you should. Sounds like you have reason enough."

Nancy and Carol roamed the room, joined one pair after another, spoke softly into the acting-facilitator's ear, suggested a word here, a phrase there. Except for bathroom/cigarette breaks, we continued the mat work until noon, reconvened at three o'clock and worked until dinner.

Saturday was a repeat of Friday. I began to identify when another's work triggered me, and it became easier to take my place on the mat. It wasn't all hitting and cursing. There were also moments when I felt sorrow, guilt, shame, even gratitude.

Unremembered moments floated to the surface. Suddenly I smelled the fresh-dug earth of Appalachia. I was holding my mother's hand and staring down at my shiny new patent-leather shoes as we stood beside the grave of my nine-month-old sister. I was barely two. I'd had no memory of her until that moment on the mat. I didn't even know her name. Now I sobbed, wordless. Great waves of guilt crashed over me. How could I have forgotten this baby sister? How could I have forgotten that at age two I was so frightened as I imagined her lying under all that dirt?

I fought to breathe.

By Saturday evening my body felt different. My neck and legs were no longer stiff, and the pain had left my shoulders. I felt at ease inside my skin. Did I now walk through a room with the ease I'd seen in Sheila and David at the LDT? I don't know. What I did know was that I had never felt so present.

*

Sunday morning I slipped back into my professional persona, emotions vaulted, lips smiling, costume a touch above what I'd wear to muck out the garage. After all, I'd be crawling around on the floor most of the day. Cups of black coffee and my usual quota of cigarettes started my engine. I was ready to greet the volunteers who would assume the role of LDT conference attendees.

The first to arrive was Sharon, my client from the Council whose husband beat her at least once a month. She denied this but I'd seen the marks. Her manner was that of a frightened kitten. Given the chance, she'd live under her bed and come out only to serve her abusive husband and four-year-old son. As if designed as victim by central casting, she was all one color: washed-out blonde hair pulled back in a low ponytail, pale complexion, dust-colored shirt and pants, brown shoes. Even her blue eyes were pale. She seldom smiled and wore no make-up. I feared if something didn't change for her she would become invisible, either by her own hands or by those of her husband.

She dipped her head in greeting. I handed her coffee that she accepted and carried to a table, where she sat looking out at the lake.

Other volunteers arrived, signed in, grabbed coffee and took seats separate from one another. All looked as if a jury had sentenced them to death. Had I looked that scared my first day at the LDT last year, or even on Friday? Just one, a stout grandmotherly woman, was all smiles and sunshine.

At nine o'clock, everyone convened in the workroom. Hesitantly I joined in on the welcome ceremony. Due to unfinished business over that second-grade teacher who told me to mouth words but not sing them, I still avoided group singing. Yet I understood the importance of this ritual. Before the singing, personal walls were almost visible; after the singing, individuals became an integrated part of a unit. A level of trust developed. Later, as an accomplished facilitator, I was able to identify when the shift happened. When Elisabeth was present, the unit seemed even more solid. Maybe this was because of the undeniable joy with which she joined in. She could rock the rafters.

Helen agreed to deliver the lecture on quadrants and did it well. A different trainee spoke of the five survival emotions. As I listened, I wondered if I would ever be able to deliver that lecture in a believable manner. I didn't fully accept the theory and found it impossible to imagine myself saying, "The pain you feel is your own. Not hers. Not his. Your own."

Was this to bar me from acceptance into Shanti Nilaya? I deeply wanted to become a facilitator who traveled with Elisabeth to exciting places like England, Australia, New Zealand, even into prisons to work with death row inmates. I yearned for the calm the staff exuded, but I also longed for the glamour I imagined their work involved— meeting people all over the globe. I wanted to leave the addiction field and travel with a world-renowned celebrity, Dr. Elisabeth Kübler-Ross, the Death and Dying Lady. Her fascination with the Angels had given me the chance, and I didn't want to blow it. But first, I needed more training.

Nancy called break and we all filed out. I bolted onto the deck for a smoke. The guinea pigs we were supposed to help milled around, took care of business and then resumed their seats. Carol asked, "Who wants to go first?" One of the trainees accepted the invitation, took her place on the mat and began work. With each whack of the hose, I saw witnesses flinch, tears well up, faces flush, shoulders climb toward ears.

Sharon looked as if she was going to faint. I tapped her shoulder and asked her to join me on one of the mats. Robot-like, she followed my instructions without question.

"Sit here," I said. She climbed onto the mat. "You can take off your shoes if you wish," I said, and she did. "Are you okay?"

"I feel sick. I'm going to throw up."

"Try to scream, that might help."

"I can't."

"Take a deep breath and on exhale, scream." She breathed deeply, opened her mouth but couldn't make a sound, not even the squeak I'd managed on my first try. What now? I could see she was scared: her skin was pale, eyes wide, the white showing all around the iris. But she was unable to release the natural reaction to her fear, the scream.

"Try again and I'll scream with you. Breathe in … one … two … three … scream!" I opened my throat and issued forth a deep lingering scream from my diaphragm, almost operatic in tone.

Sharon managed a pitiful soft whine.

"That's great, try again." I was amazed at her willingness. I had fought against even trying to scream when I was first on a mat, but she was giving it her all. On her second try, the sound was louder, but still only throat deep.

"I feel better, I think," she said.

"Good. Now let's try the hose." I repeated the directions Nancy had given me yesterday: "Both hands, over the head, and straight down onto the books, no side to side motion, that's dangerous." To my ears I sounded confident, knowledgeable.

I was shocked to discover I wasn't acting. It was as if I'd said those words thousands of times.

Bam!

"Again."

Bam!

"Again. Now use words."

She froze in mid-strike. "What should I say?"

"It doesn't matter. Whatever comes up. Cursing is okay. Anything. A sound, anything."

No response from Sharon. She sat stone still, hands in her lap, staring at me. What was I to do now? I pulled from my first time here on the mat. "Say stop." I put the hose into her limp hands again.

Her fingers closed around it. Arms went up and whack! Three more strikes before she managed a whispered, "Stop." The word didn't burst her dam as it had mine, but she kept whacking. "My arms are tired. Is that enough?" Tears filled her eyes.

I wanted to cry as well. I'd failed. I lacked the skill to push her from victim to anger.

"I didn't do it right, did I?"

What was I to say? No, you didn't do it right? You made me look like a fool? Instead, I repeated what Nancy had said to me. "You did just fine. Why the tears?"

"I'm scared. If he hurts Jason, I'm afraid I'll kill him."

Oh, boy. I was in way over my head. I looked around for Nancy or Carol, but both were across the room with their backs to me. "Has he hurt Jason before?"

"No. I make sure he's in bed before Henry gets home."

"How would you do that? Kill him?"

"I'd choke him. Kick him."

I handed her the large bath towel from beside the mat. "Show me how you'd do that."

She grabbed the folded towel and began twisting it while I played anchor from the other end. My finger got pinched in a fold and I almost let go. If I had, she'd have gone flying over backward onto the floor, such was the energy with which she choked the towel. Her neck reddened from its base to the top of her face. Her lips drew back in a grimace, exposing her teeth. A growl issued from her throat. Mousey, meek Sharon had transformed into a crazed killer. I had no doubt she was capable of murder, and I wanted to cheer her on.

She stood up suddenly. "I want to kick him too."

I stood as well. "You'll have to use words," I said and directed her to kick the sides of the mat.

Sharon, who flinched if anyone said shit in her presence, let loose with a string of curse words that made me proud. Was this kicking okay? Nothing like this had happened before. I caught Nancy's eye. She nodded and started my way. Before she reached us, Sharon had run down and was sitting on the mat. Nancy said nothing, just squatted, listened for a moment, then moved on.

Sharon giggled. "That felt good. Can I hit him some more?"

I restacked the damaged, almost shredded, books, handed her the hose and leaned back out of her striking range.

"Die. Die. Die. Fucker! I hate you."

Joyful laughter bubbled in my gut.

CHAPTER FOURTEEN
Jason and the Raisins

AFTER THE TRAINING WEEKEND, another "re-entry" into real life. I returned to work on Monday morning. It felt like lake-walking in early spring, the most dangerous time to set foot on frozen bodies of water. Casual chit-chat with co-workers was an exercise in slipping around questions about my weekend. People asked, Did Jerry and you go somewhere romantic? Did he cook for you again? Did you have a fight? Is that why you aren't talking?

Whenever the boss's office called for me, I broke into a terrified sweat. Had he found out about the boundary I'd violated? It was seriously unethical to meet with Council clients outside the office; if he learned that I'd worked with Sharon and two other of the Council's female clients at the training retreat, I'd be fired. Even worse, an ethics complaint would bar me from working in any field of counseling anywhere. Until I could travel the globe with Elisabeth and Shanti Nilaya, I needed to keep my job. What had I been I thinking? As my mother would have said, I knew better! I couldn't even blame the Angels. I'd created this mess myself.

Two weeks passed with no indication that I was in trouble. Evidently the women I'd worked with held my secret, but why didn't any of them come into the Council for an appointment? Call me? Anything? Why hadn't at least one let me know how she was doing?

I didn't dare call them. I was too afraid. I'd heard that someone from the first LDT I'd attended ended up in a psych ward afterwards. What if one of my women had gone home and flipped out? Or, worse, committed a violent act? When I needed the Angels the most, it seemed they'd deserted me too. No whisperings, no writings to direct me, no comforting words.

I was alone.

September First arrived, the opening day of moose hunting season. The air was crisp, and coffee tasted more wonderful than it had since this time last year. What could beat the smell and taste of fresh coffee on the first cold morning of fall? The governor should make this a coffee drinker's holiday.

Those were my thoughts as I drove to work. After three weeks, I'd given up the fear of being fired. All was quiet.

I was on my third cup of coffee when pale, frightened Sharon from the workshop breezed into the Council, all smiles and sunshine, little Jason at her side. Luckily I saw her before anyone else did and hurried her into my office before she uttered a word.

"What's the hurry?" she asked. "I wasn't going to say anything. I know the risk you took." She sat, legs outstretched. Four-year-old Jason leaned against her thigh and she stroked his back. Today her monotone pants, shirt and boots looked carefully chosen and stylish, and her blond hair hung loose. She even wore make-up. But more than a dab of make-up had to account for the transformation I observed—the tilt of her head, or maybe the way she looked me in the eye, or was it that she was smiling?

My hands itched to grab Sharon by the shoulders and shake her senseless. Instead, I said, evenly, "I've been worried. You didn't call. You didn't come in for your appointment."

"A lot has happened." Jason looked up, and she smiled at him and smoothed his hair, the same pale blonde as hers. "I'm sorry."

"You could've called."

"Actually, I couldn't. Henry ripped out the phone line, and the phone company won't be out to repair it until Friday."

"Oh, my." I felt weak, my anger spent. Was that why she hadn't come for her appointment? He'd beaten her and she'd waited for the bruises to fade? Was that why she wore make-up? "What happened?"

"It's okay. He didn't hit me this time."

I lifted my eyebrow. How many times had I heard that one?

"No. Really," Sharon said. "He came home drunk the week before, but I was asleep. Jason and I had gone to bed at our regular time like you said to do." Hearing his name, Jason looked up. "I woke up, of course, when I heard him thrashing around in the living room, but I didn't get up or try to quiet him. I lay in bed thinking that could be me he's throwing around. And I decided—never again."

"He didn't drag you out of bed?"

"No, he just beat up the living room furniture and passed out on the floor."

Through the window behind Sharon, I watched a car speed into the parking lot and screech to a stop in the space a sidewalk's width from my desk. A newspaper headline flashed inside my brain: Angry Husband Drives Through Office Window, kills wife and counselor.

"Like you said," she was saying, "I didn't even try to put him to bed. Just let him sleep where he fell. It was so easy; don't know why I didn't do it before."

I wanted to laugh. All my preaching had finally sunk in, but why now? "Why is the phone ripped out of the wall?"

"The next morning I told Henry if he came home drunk and broke anything or hit me I'd call the police. Last Friday he showed up drunk and mean." Never before, except at the LDT training, had Sharon admitted her husband was violent. "I took Jason into the bedroom, locked the door and called 911. He must have heard me talking because there was a crash, like something hit the kitchen wall and the phone went dead. The operator already had the address, and before he could break into the bedroom the police arrived."

"Are you and Jason safe?"

She nodded. "He was hauled off to jail." Her voice was muffled as she dug in her sack-purse, came up with a mini-box of raisins and handed them to Jason. "I filed charges and swore out an order of protection. And, besides, my sister's coming to stay with us. That'll keep him away better than the police. He hates my sister."

She let Jason feed her a raisin, and I drank in the sight of mother and child. "I came in to say thank you," she said. "Without the retreat I think I might be in jail by now."

"For what?"

"For shooting him."

"I thought you wanted to choke and kick him."

"I was just being nice. Didn't want to shock you. I'd planned to use the revolver he keeps in the nightstand. If I had, where'd I be now?"

I let out my breath. "Oh my. Yes, indeed, where would you be?"

*

Before the training sessions, I'd had many questions. After them, I had more.

On the mat, during the first training weekend, I'd pounded my ex several times and screamed my rebuttal to his assaults. My white-hot rage cauterized wounds I didn't know I had, burned away hurt and shame, healed scars I carried from my ten-year marriage to a womanizing-alcoholic who had battered me. Although I'd divorced him six years earlier, my anger felt as fresh as it should have been the first time he hit me.

Is this what happened for Sharon as well?

I needed to know more.

Before the workshop and mat training, I primarily depended on the Twelve Steps I taught to my clients. They'd helped to salvage many lives. The basics were sound: We admit we are powerless; we believe a Power greater than ourselves can restore us; we turn our will and lives over to this Power; we do a fearless self-inventory and admit our wrongs to the Power, ourselves and others; we become ready for that Power to remove our defects and shortcomings; we list those whom we've harmed and make amends whenever possible; we continue personal inventory and admission of wrongs; we achieve spiritual awakening and carry this learning to other addicted people.

I knew these powerful steps changed lives, but why? I needed to understand, yet it seemed I was the only one who wanted an explanation.

I didn't believe that a magical being called God—or, as AA said, a "Higher Power"—rearranged individual lives. There had to be another reason why the steps worked. My own life had changed, but I didn't believe a superior being paid much attention to my affairs. I had the Angel thing going, but I didn't exactly believe in them either. I wanted explanations; I wanted science. I'd thought Elisabeth would give me those answers. So far she hadn't. She claimed to be a scientist, but I hadn't heard much science from her.

Doubts crept in.

The Twelve Steps worked, though, and so did mat-work. But how did cursing, screaming, and beating up phone books make changes in people? The changes Sharon made were real and could be long-lasting. She was divorcing her abusive husband after years of not being able to do so. What happened on the mat to give her that strength?

I wanted Elisabeth to answer my questions, but when I asked she said, "Do your own work." That was always her answer. When I'd asked her things in person at the LDT, she'd punctuated the statement with a pat on my arm.

Now I began phoning her, asking every time, "How do I learn what happens on the mat? How do I learn to facilitate others?"

"Do you own work."

"That's not enough. I'm not that smart."

At the end of every phone call, she added, "Long time you send me no yellow pages." I tried not to squirm under those requests for Angel writings that I didn't have.

The phone calls from terminally ill patients and their families continued too. I still held support meetings in my home and parroted Elisabeth's words. Health-care providers considered these meetings as training for their own work. Because I was the only one in the local area doing this, no one questioned me. After all, I'd met Elisabeth Kübler-Ross, the famous doctor of death and dying. People believed me to be an authority. Only I knew the truth: I had no answers.

"Do your own work," Elisabeth demanded. So for the next two years, work I did.

I checked out psychology textbooks from the library and read them cover to cover. I read self-help books by all the popular theorists. I attended lectures. I ordered audio tapes. I re-read all of Elisabeth's books. I studied primal scream therapy and Gestalt, which Elisabeth utilized in mat therapy.

Sheila sent me audio tapes that described the Prison Project, in which Elisabeth took an LDT inside a prison and worked with convicted murderers and rapists—matted them, actually. Afterward, the guards reported changed behavior in the inmates who had participated. One, a few years later, gained parole because his behavior changed from consistently violent to consistently non-violent. He credited Elisabeth's LDT as his turning point.

*

During those two years, I also scheduled and participated in two more training weekends with Shanti Nilaya and attended three workshops with Gregg Furth, Ph.D. He'd taught for seven years at the Jungian Institute in Zürich. I was enamored with Furth because of the way he answered questions. Never did he say simply yes or no. He invited the questioner on a journey rich in myth and symbolism. Best of all, he didn't say, as Elisabeth always did, "Do your own work." He led his workshop students in experiential exercises where we made discoveries and gained insights.

Through Furth, I learned to interpret spontaneous drawings and conduct psychodrama scenarios. I later applied what I'd learned to counseling sessions, both at home and with selected clients at my job. Interpreting my clients' drawings led to breakthroughs and even, in one case, saved a life.

[Years later (in 2002), Furth's book *The Secret World of Drawings: A Jungian Approach to Healing Through Art* (Studies in Jungian Psychology by Jungian Analysts #99) was published with an introduction by Elisabeth.]

The other wonderful thing I gained through working with Furth was that he shed some light on my Angels! He explained that according to

Jungian theory there is a Collective Unconscious whose patterns have existed through all human cultures and times. These patterns contain knowledge that can guide and complete the human experience; they are our road to "wholeness and individuation". Dreams and active imagination are the main carriers between ourselves and the Collective Unconscious.

"So," he told me, "your Angels could be messengers from the depths of the Collective Unconscious. That explains your automatic writing. It looks like you can suspend your ego and just let the messages come naturally, as your hand writes them. They aren't part of your conscious mind."

I was so relieved to hear these ideas. How perfectly my Angels fit inside Jung's mystical framework!

*

My research into all things psychological began to adversely affect my work at the Council. During the day, I preached AA doctrine, but AA theory was anti-psychology. Twelve- Step Programs of the early 1980s taught that psychiatry didn't work, was all phony-baloney. They called psychiatrists pill-pushers who were responsible for millions becoming addicted to prescription drugs.

There was some truth in that, but I knew there were reputable therapists and sound psychotherapies that helped people break through to better lives. AA was not the end-all of help for alcoholics and their families. I saw this to be especially true with the abused women and terrified children who sought help from my family program.

Because I was "doing my own work," as Elizabeth demanded, I was experiencing psychological insights into my behavior that gave me choices—where before I'd only reacted. I could no longer truthfully tell my clients that AA was enough, that there was no help beyond the Twelve Steps. Yet when my clients asked, "Is this all?" I wasn't allowed to refer them to psychotherapy.

As my knowledge increased, this restriction became unbearable. I began breaking rules. I met clients in my home and did mat work with them. I walked in fear of being found out and fired. What was I really doing for, or to, these people?

CHAPTER FIFTEEN
G-Force of Liftoff

"MOM, JERRY'S HERE," Christine, who was now seventeen, yelled from the living room.

I wondered what could have kept him; he was twenty minutes late. The reservation clerk had said, "Be at the airport an hour before departure time." Because I hate to rush, I had tacked on another hour and forty-five minutes, just in case on the one-hour trip from Wasilla to Anchorage we found black ice on the Glenn Highway, an accident on the bridge, or a moose in the flats south of town. Alaskan roads were always uncertain, and I couldn't bear it if I missed my plane.

This trip represented a lifetime of longing, years of saving vacation time, a full year of planning, and months of second-guessing every purchase. Before a dollar left my fist, I'd ask myself, Do I really need this haircut now? Can I get another year out of this jacket? Shall I eat out or run home for lunch? My Alaska dividend check had paid for the plane fare, but there would be other expenses; I'd be traveling around England for two weeks on my own after the two LDTs I was scheduled to work. Last week at the bank, even as I signed my name on traveler's checks, I'd found the journey impossible to believe.

In London I'd have my final examination before being accepted as a facilitator with The Elisabeth Kübler-Ross Foundation that had created Shanti-Nalaya and other services. The workshops would mark the summation of months of training in the externalization process. I would facilitate two workshops under Elisabeth's direct supervision. Though only one workshop was required to complete my training, I'd been accepted for two. In the first, I would serve as a trainee; in the second, for the first time, I would be a graduate facilitator and be paid for my contribution.

I couldn't get my mind around the idea that I, who was raised a hillbilly in Kentucky's Appalachia, could actually travel to Europe. My

Dad's brothers only went overseas during WWII. They came back nervous and secretive, their naturally thin faces pinched. We kids learned quickly not to speak when approaching them from behind; otherwise, we might be knocked down. It took only once to learn that lesson.

I remember one time Grandma shooed us out of the room. Being curious and inventive children, we listened from under the dining room window and heard Uncle Dan say, "Those are real bones. The piles were higher than a man standing." A few days later, my two cousins and I found where he'd hidden those eight-by-ten black and white glossies that showed piles of human skeletons.

I've wondered since if that was the reason they never traveled again. If sights such as those were out there, they probably thought it was better to stay home. My father was the only one of thirteen children to move his family out of Kentucky. Most of my aunts, uncles, and cousins lived all their lives without indoor plumbing and would die without crossing a state line.

Yet I had already crossed many state lines, and now I was about to cross the Atlantic! That is, if Jerry didn't make me miss my flight.

"I have only these two," I said, shoving my suitcases out the door before he had time to mount the steps.

"Hello to you too," he said, taking my carry-on.

"What happened? You're late."

"We've plenty of time." He walked s-l-o-w-l-y to his car and painstakingly arranged my two bags in the trunk. I wanted to scream, "Hustle! Step lively. At least look like you're making an effort." But women in my family didn't scream at their men. I busied myself hugging the kids and saying those last minute things a mother says when leaving her teenage children home alone for a month with only casual supervision from adult friends.

"Yadda, yadda, yadda. Just go, Mom," would have been their good-bye words if they'd spoken their true feelings, but each in turn said, "I love you, Mom. We'll be fine. Have fun."

As we backed out of the driveway, I had to ask, "What happened? You were supposed to be here a half-hour ago."

"The plane won't leave without you."

I would later discover that Jerry has an unusual contempt for airlines, their schedules and restrictions. Why this is so, I don't know. It's as if he was engaged in a private war with them. His battle strategy is to board at the very last minute. His one true victory came when a plane bound for Barrow was called back to the terminal. Its doors opened and its steps came down. The plane waited as he alone, luggage in hand, walked (I'm sure unhurriedly) across the tarmac and boarded.

I tried to convince him this time was different. "This is an international flight on a 747, Not some commuter flight you take to Ketchikan or Yakutat. This one won't wait." He was not persuaded.

I tried a different tactic. "In all my years in Alaska, no one's ever been stopped for speeding."

He countered with statistics: "Excessive speed doesn't alter arrival time by more than five minutes. Not worth the risk."

"What risk? We're the only car on the road."

"They're called accidents because they are accidents," he quoted, and continued at an infuriating fifty-miles-an-hour. We eventually arrived at Anchorage International with only fifteen minutes to spare. While we kissed good-bye at the jet-way entrance I'm sure he was thinking—Jerry one-hundred percent, airlines zero. To my embarrassment, I was the last passenger to board.

*

Strapped into my seat, waiting for take-off, I had an epiphany: I was going to die.

Since this journey meant my impossible childhood dream was coming true, my life was ending. It had begun back in first grade while playing "London Bridge is Falling Down". A friend and I would build a bridge by extending our arms overhead and locking fingers; then our classmates would file between us as we sang the song. When it ended, we'd drop our arms and capture "my fair lady." From that time forward I told myself, "Someday, I'm going to London," but in my heart I'd believed I wouldn't.

I had no sense of life after this trip. As I accepted a blanket and pillow from the flight attendant, I concluded I had to either come up with a new impossible-to-achieve-dream, or die. I tried to send my mind into the future and envision my children's graduations from high school, their marriages, my grandchildren. Nothing. I tried to come up with a substitute dream but discarded ideas one after another. Traveling to England was monumental. I could imagine nothing grander.

The pilot dimmed the interior lights and started the plane speeding toward liftoff. "Welcome aboard Japan Airline's flight from

Tokyo to Heathrow." Would this monster jet crash into Cook Inlet? Everyone knew these bumble bees were too big to fly.

In those moments before gaining altitude, I wasn't frightened. I thought of my children. If I died, they'd miss me, but would survive. They'd live with my parents in Arizona because their father lacked the skill or interest to parent. Money wouldn't be a problem; I'd bought travel insurance.

Did I worry about my soul? The afterlife? No.

Due to my upbringing in a God-fearing/charismatic religion, the daughter of a preacher, I'd struggled for years wondering which was the true religious or spiritual path. Though I came from a family that didn't read books or magazines, I'd become a voracious reader myself. So far, in my search for spiritual truth, I'd read from the *Koran*, *The Book of Mormon*, the *Bible* (different editions and translations), *The Watchtower*, *Religions of the Eastern World*, and *Psychic Phenomenon Behind the Iron Curtain*. I'd listened to tapes. I'd read about pagan rituals and dipped into journals on spiritualism. I wondered about Judaism, Catholicism, and Hinduism. I'd practiced yoga and spent a day locked in my bedroom contemplating whether swatting a mosquito did permanent harm to my soul. I studied with the Coptic Foundation and the

White Brotherhood. Reincarnation answered my questions about why babies were born with disabilities and evil was sometimes rewarded and the virtuous punished. Now I had to wonder if those were real answers.

Thank God I'd discarded the concepts of a heaven with golden avenues and a hell with fires that roasted souls throughout eternity, or I might have lost my mind completely. Even so, by age thirty-five I'd worked myself into a state of panic and then into clinical depression.

My salvation came the day I walked to the bookshelves, gathered my books on and about the soul, and threw them into the trash. I had developed my own answer: I'd treat companions in this life as kindly as I am able, and I'd let the afterlife take care of itself. I resolved to do no harm. (Mosquitoes, insects, and food animals excluded.)

From that day forward, I refused to give my attention to any subject remotely related to the soul or the metaphysical. I walked away when others started discussing these subjects. I refused to delve into anything that was not of the here and now. I didn't attend church or religious study groups.

Surprisingly, my life became simpler. I stopped trying to buy prosperity with tithes and had money to pay my bills on time. The time I had spent reading I now used to clean house.

Parenting became fun. Friends and I talked about novels, kids, and recipes.

That was the simple life I had lived for several years before the Angels intruded and re-complicated things. That's another reason why they were so unwelcome. They forced me back into wondering about the metaphysical and the paranormal. Angels confused me!

As I felt the G-force of liftoff, I reconciled myself to my life's end. No Angels contradicted me. I wondered if the plane would go down before we reached England, or crash on landing, or if I'd perish in a freak accident or illness while in Great Britain. I hoped catastrophe would wait for the return flight, because seated in the rear was a group of Japanese school children.

If the return flight was destined to crash, that would explain Jerry's last-minute refusal to join me after my work was concluded and we could spend two weeks of touring before flying home together. I had already bought my ticket, and the arrangements for me to facilitate two workshops with Elisabeth were locked in solid, when one night—as Jerry served salmon steaks he'd caught and cooked—he dropped the bomb: "I can't join you in London. I don't know why, I just can't go."

He would not be moved. He denied having a reason, only that he had a feeling in his gut so powerful he couldn't oppose it. I'd never known a man who admitted to having a feeling, let alone acted on one, especially when he knew his action would meet resistance from me. What defense did I have against a feeling? None.

I'd had weeks to adjust to his decision, but his change of plans still felt like a betrayal. However, now that I was to die on this flight it made sense. Though we weren't married and didn't live together, we were a couple. If he wouldn't be on the return flight with me when it crashed, I could count on him to be there to help my kids get to my parents. Alone in the darkened plane, this made sense to me.

I relaxed against the pressure of the seatbelt and closed my eyes. A strange sensation enveloped me. It took a while to realize it was the feeling of being alone. I was not daughter, sister, lover, or mother. I was autonomous. Never had I felt so free.

My seat companion, a young Japanese woman, turned to me as the plane leveled off. "May I exercise my English with you?" She repeated her question twice before I understood her.

"Sure," I said.

"My brother has paid for this trip for me. He said to take my English abroad to gain confidence." She spoke with much repeating and rephrasing. We ordered drinks and settled down. I thought we would exchange life stories, but that was not the case. I listened, she talked.

"After the big bomb our country was devastated. Our wise leaders saw we had to make a new plan. We are to conquer the world by commerce."

I almost choked on an ice cube, but she was as composed as if she'd shared a recipe for steamed rice. "It is my national obligation, you see." As she explained, I felt as if she were telling me things her countrymen wouldn't want her to disclose. What if I were a spy? She said that all students studied English from pre-school up; every child was required to speak fluent English and learn business. Her brothers were in banking and lived abroad in their service to Japan. I sipped my Tanqueray and tonic and looked around to see who else was listening.

I'd seen this trip as the end of an educational cycle. I hadn't known it also would mark the beginning of my education as a citizen of the world.

CHAPTER SIXTEEN
My British Knight

My KNIGHT-IN-SHINING-ARMOR wasn't wearing chain mail when he rescued me. He only wore a cap and an ordinary shirt tucked into his trousers. No white stallion either; his ride was a shiny black London taxi. He spoke with a Scottish accent and called me Luv.

On that day in 1983, Heathrow Airport was as impossible for me to leave as an ancient tower under a King's guard.

I had been on the ground for less than an hour when I was accosted by a Customs Agent. He didn't welcome me into his country as I'd expected, just belched whiskey breath into my face and refused to understand a word I said. His simple question "Business or pleasure?" turned into a shouting match. He accused me of being ignorant or perhaps criminal. The problem was I hadn't memorized the abbey's name where the LDT was to be held. Had I known my eventual destination was important, I'd have made the effort. The brochure I dug from my purse served as a magic sword to slay this oaf and his objections. A sniff and a head jerk signaled his surrender. I'd have preferred blood.

Triumphant, I strolled down the ramp past protesters holding small signs. Where I'd expected to see "Nix to Nukes" or "Ban the Bomb" were words like "Fukushima" and "Gunma." I should have seen these strange signs as an omen that I'd entered into a world unknown to me. Unaware, I proceeded with confidence to an information booth. My presentation was perfect: head up, eye contact, smile planted firmly on my lips. I asked about public transportation that would get me to the address I presented. The pretty, uniformed woman behind the counter spoke clearly. I heard every word, but Hatton Cross, the tube, Charing Cross, and Heathrow to Gatwick meant nothing to me.

I smiled, thanked her, and turned away. I tried three other booths with the same result before I realized I was trapped inside Heathrow Airport, held hostage by ignorance and lack of preparation.

I needed nourishment, or at least a place to sit down and decide my next move. I found the food court but no gratification. No coffee pot in sight. I looked everywhere for the little squat glass-pot one needed only to lift and pour to refuel. I found instead a monstrous stainless steel contraption with multiple levers and spouts. Fear alone kept me from being scalded.

The vending machines were less frightening but no more helpful because I didn't know which coins to use. Defeated, I found a corner between the food court and bathrooms and sat on my suitcase, barely feeling the handle bite into my butt. I sat, face in hands, and cried.

Finally, cried out and much relieved, I slipped into the bathroom for a quick touch-up. As I wiped mascara smears off my cheeks, I asked my reflection where those damn Angels were when I needed them.

At that moment, the word *Taxi* was breathed into my left ear. Did I imagine it or had the Angels actually come when called? A taxi! What a great idea, though perhaps pricey. After careful consideration, I decided anything less than fifty American dollars would be worth it. Thus began my love affair with London cabbies.

My white knight, Malcolm, asked, "First time in London, Luv?"

His tone was friendly, and he looked and sounded familiar, akin to my Appalachian uncles in the Kentucky hills. Like them, he had pale blue eyes and a shock of black hair. Most surprising was his accent: he spoke the dialect of my childhood. Malcolm was a lively version of my heritage, which was, as my father proclaimed, Scot-Irish, heavy on the Scot.

Best of all, Malcolm spoke words I understood. His question sounded like genuine interest, and I left no detail unexplained. I told him about my training with Elisabeth Kübler-Ross. I gave him a recap of her career, told of her travels and her celebrity, and pressed upon him my excitement to be visiting in his England. It would be another two weeks before I learned how Scots felt about Jolly Old England.

The day was gray with a soft drizzle that edged toward rain by the time Malcolm parked at the curb in front of the address I'd given him. It seemed to be a house. I thought the address I had was for an abbey. Although only mid-afternoon, it felt much later. I'd been awake for almost twenty-four hours and my stomach reminded me that my last meal had been breakfast on the plane.

Malcolm suggested I go up and knock on the door while he waited at the curb. When he said "go up," he meant exactly that. I didn't count, but

I'm sure there were at least fifteen steps. I insisted he just drop me. I'd taken up too much of his time already, and he'd even refused my offered tip. His expression turned sour, but he brought my luggage up the steep steps and left my suitcases and me standing at door. He retreated to his cab but didn't drive off.

Deep woofing sounds from inside answered my knock. No cute little poodles or terriers these. I knocked again and the door bowed outward from the force of the dogs charging from the inside. I stepped backwards and almost fell off the stoop. I felt nauseous. Big dogs have been a phobia of mine since childhood. My Knight was beside me before I'd recovered my equilibrium. He said not a word, simply picked up my luggage and put it back in the cab. I followed, head down and tears stinging my eyes.

We sat and watched the rain. Finally I said, "I have the phone number where Elisabeth is staying. Maybe I should call her."

Malcolm said, "If we can find a box that works. Kids these days find pleasure in destroying property." He stopped at four red phone booths before he found one that worked. He used his own coin and dialed, then handed the phone to me. It rang and rang. No one answered. "What now, Luv?"

My Knight suggested an affordable hotel within walking distance to cafés and drove me there, carried my luggage, and helped me register. When I asked about a place to eat, he looked at his shoes. "Nothing open 'til tea time at four." I felt faint. "Come on, Luv, get back in the cab. I have a friend. He owns a restaurant near here. Maybe he can find a scrap in the kitchen to feed one starving American. You like Indian food, Luv?"

"Anything. I'm not choosy." He drove a short distance and left me in the cab while he pounded on the rear door of a small unlighted building. The door opened and a dark-skinned man wearing an apron stepped out. Malcolm talked. The man shook his head no. Malcolm pointed at me. The man's mouth tightened and he shook his head. Malcolm gestured, arms flying. The man looked in my direction, back at Malcolm and grimaced. Malcolm smiled and motioned for me to come in.

I was seated without ceremony or menu at a small table. Malcolm explained that his friend was worried he'd get in trouble for selling food outside regular business hours. A plate of lumpy brown paste and rice was set in front of me. It was spicy but I ate every spoonful. When I tried to pay, the proprietor refused. I guessed it was okay to give food away or serve a friend but not a paying customer. That was the first and most memorable of many mystery meals I was to eat while in England.

My hunger subdued, I walked to my hotel. I missed Malcolm. To him I'm sure I was just another fare, but he'll always be my knight-in-shining-armor, so kind and proper. I'd been single for six years and the men I usually met wanted more from me than I was willing to give. Not Malcolm. He got me safely housed and fed without one inappropriate gesture. My thanks to Sir Malcolm, wherever he is.

When I got back to my room, I fell face down on the bed and slept.

So ended the first day of living my impossible England dream: in the wrong place, separated from all things familiar, even language. If I'd known it would be like this, would I have left home?

*

The next day was Sunday. I slept in and almost missed the hotel's breakfast. Not having traveled outside the USA, except to drive through Canada on my way to Alaska, I was unprepared for the differences of everyday implements and customs. The forceful peeling away of my American cocksureness began at breakfast, with toast.

Toast should be served hot, stacked on a plate and saturated with melted butter. Not dry and suspended on a metal rack to air-cool before being placed on the table. How was one to butter cold toast? I settled for jam. Accepting cold toast was a stretch, but it was coffee that pushed me outside my cultural norms. After my first cup of English coffee, I became (and remain) a confirmed tea drinker, with cream in the English style.

I didn't transition into a cosmopolitan traveler over one cup of coffee, though. I'd traveled to England with an intact picture of who I was and how I should behave, and I thought I'd never need to re-evaluate that picture. I hadn't known that my self-assessment was accurate only as long as I remained inside my cultural fortress, the western US of A. Nor did I know how lost I would be once removed from my personal realm. If I'd traveled with a companion, we'd have created a two-person outpost of home and laughed at calling knee-high rubber boots Wellies instead of break-up boots as we knew them in Alaska. We'd laugh at references to sweaters as jumpers, and I'd have remained unchallenged inside the safety of my friend's opinion of me. England wouldn't have penetrated my cultural shield. As it was, I was alone. England touched me.

CHAPTER SEVENTEEN
Warm English Gin

THE RAIN kept me confined to the hotel most of Sunday, but today, the first day of the LDT, dawned clear and sunny. I was rested and fed. I practically ran up the abbey steps, followed by a different, but equally kind, taxi driver who carried my luggage. (London black-taxi drivers are a national treasure.) My excitement at having finally arrived at my destination was such a thrill that I hardly noticed the red brick, four-hundred-year-old abbey with its high ceilings, stained glass windows and hardwood floors.

Elisabeth tackled me five feet inside the entrance. "Jan's here. We found her!" she yelled, giving me a squeeze.

I was mobbed. The staff abandoned their registration duties to shower me with hugs and welcomes. Elisabeth was the only person I recognized, and she made brief introductions: Stephen, a doctor from New York, Bernard from Germany, Gisele from Switzerland—all members of Elisabeth's loosely constructed international team. Volunteer members of the London-based Shanti Nilaya Support Group, the ones responsible for organizing the workshop, joined the cluster. A tall sharp-nosed man said, "We missed you at the airport. What happened?"

"Yes. Peter met your flight," Elisabeth said.

"And the next three flights from the U.S. as well," a disembodied voice added.

No one had told me I'd be met. I wasn't surprised. Misinformation or no information at all was the norm when it came to communication from the home office. The hiring procedures of this organization were anything but corporate. It was run by zealous volunteers who worshiped Elisabeth because of the changes they'd experienced due to her intervention, but many had no experience at the jobs they were doing and little or no training. To me, with my background in accounting, this disorganization was both scary and miraculous.

"Where have you been?" a stout woman asked.

"When you didn't show up at the Campbell's, we didn't know where to look."

"Why you not telephone?" Elisabeth asked.

When I was finally allowed to speak I explained I'd gone to the address given and been greeted by a locked door and large dogs. I'd called the number Elisabeth gave me but no one answered. Why I didn't call on Sunday went unexplained. They didn't need to know the British phone system had me cowed, and the idea of asking for assistance from the hotel clerk gave me chills.

Fiona solved the mystery: "Everyone was at hospital."

Doug Campbell (whose home I was to have stayed at over the weekend) had taken his wife Patricia to the hospital because she'd gone into early labor with their first child. Their neighbor, Peter, had volunteered to meet me at the airport, and the rest of the staff kept Doug company. Peter and I missed each other at Heathrow because I didn't know to look for my name among the "protest" signs.

Gisele said, "You're lodged next to me. Come, I'll show you the way." Two words describe Gisele: solid and purposeful. She did a military pivot and marched toward an exit. Her hard leather shoes bounced echoes off walls and ceiling. I struggled to keep up. My shoulder purse slipped to my elbow and I almost tripped battling my oversized suitcase. It had small wheels and seemed designed to fall over. One purchase I'd gotten right—my black, rubber-soled Naturalizer walking shoes. My hurried steps whispered through the long halls under arches and down narrow steps to a nun's cell in the basement.

The room where I'd spend the week had a slit window high in the brick wall above the single bed on which a thin mattress lay on coil-springs. A small bedside table held a lamp and a Bible. I felt I'd stepped into a medieval monk's cell. Did I mention the thin, scratchy wool blanket? Excitement bubbled through me; I was truly in the England of my imagination.

I asked Gisele for directions to the bathroom and learned the difference between a bathroom and a toilet. She took me to a large cold room with curtained stalls; behind each curtain was an enameled bathtub perched on claw feet beside which stood a small stool. It would be weeks before "where's the loo?" would roll off my tongue without me feeling I was playing a child's game and speaking in code.

*

Staff, myself included, sat beside Elisabeth when she opened the workshop. As usual, she retold childhood stories about being a triplet raised by a stingy (her word) Swiss father. She told her Black Bunny story, which brought the expected tears and worked its magic, bonding participants through a shared emotional response: pain.

To my relief, I was unmoved by her words or the tears of participants. I figured this meant I'd accomplished closure on some unfinished business. During my year-long training, I'd attended intensive externalization workshops as required. The workshops were three-day affairs where experienced facilitators guided trainees in "processing personal unfinished business by using externalization"—mat work with hose and phone books. Elisabeth believed trainees learned to facilitate others by freeing ourselves of our own negative emotional memories. When asked, "How do we learn to help others?" she'd say, "Do your own work, honey."

The wisdom of Elisabeth's method is in this [edited] mission statement of Shanti Nilaya:

The Elisabeth Kübler-Ross Center Shanti Nilaya is a non-profit organization dedicated to the promotion of the concept of unconditional love as an attainable ideal. Our purpose is to spread knowledge and understanding of this concept with its underlying premises as we accept full responsibility for all of our feelings, thoughts, actions and choices. As we, in a safe environment, release negative emotions that we repressed in the past, we can live free, happy and loving lives at peace with ourselves and others. Our goal is to live this message and to spread it far and wide.

Each trainee had to sign a commitment to live by these principles, not just to their own satisfaction but also to the satisfaction of other staff members. Unfinished business ("negative repressed emotions from past experiences") become apparent through "inappropriate responses to current stimulus." It takes experience to become aware of one's own unfinished business, we were taught. In the beginning we had to have feedback from others. In the trainee's case, feedback came from staff members who'd done their own work.

What I learned while trying to live up to this high ideal was that each time I visited the mat, I experienced less pain. I could sit with the parent of a dying child and feel empathy; I could be present and hear her pain and frustration. But I was not in pain. Had it been otherwise, my career as a counselor/facilitator would have been short.

After the Black Bunny story, Elisabeth called for a physiological (loo) break. Participants left the room red-eyed and sniffing. Elisabeth and I stepped out for a cigarette. She passed me her lighter and said, "I not receive yellow written material for months. Do the Angels have nothing more to say to me?"

With my first exhale, I breathed out frustration at what I perceived was my being demoted from almost fully-trained facilitator to Angel-messenger. Was Elisabeth serious about my training, or were the Angels the only reason she kept me around? I wanted to kick something, anything. I lied: "I'll check later." In truth, I seldom consulted the Angels for Elisabeth these days. I wanted her to value me for myself, not for the Angels.

The day progressed on schedule: introduction of participants, spontaneous drawings, dismissal after dinner, staff meeting in Elisabeth's quarters. I got lost between the dining hall and my room, but a nun in flowing black redirected me. Her face was as angelic as nuns in the movies, and her voice was musical. She knew without asking that I was American, and she said she'd traveled there once to attend a teaching conference. I shrank inside my Levis and Shanti Nilaya tee shirt; even nuns traveled more than I did. But she hadn't traveled to Alaska, and she asked, "Is it really dark for six months?"

Everyone I'd met, except the customs agent, had been polite, asked the right questions, and offered non-intrusive comments that made me squirm with guilt. Every time I opened my mouth I inserted my foot clear up to my knee. At dinner, when a companion commented that she didn't watch much TV, I'd answered, "Well, no wonder. British TV is boring." The sudden silence of my tablemates told me I'd made a fool of myself—again.

I'd come to that conclusion about TV from watching an episode of "East End" at the hotel bar while sipping a warm gin and tonic. (I'd answered "Yes" to "Do you want ice?" but the bartender couldn't chip away enough frost to free the ice tray.) As I watched the British soap opera, I judged it as lukewarm as my drink. The crises these ordinary actors addressed, from a set as unglamorous as my own apartment, were alcoholism and the prospect of getting a job—nowhere near as exciting and fast-paced as "Who shot JR?" on "Dallas."

When would I learn not to share every thought that entered my head?

*

I was the last to arrive at Elisabeth's room, and based on the dense layer of cigarette smoke, it'd taken longer than I'd thought to create my face. That morning I'd applied my best face—the one complete with foundation, concealer, powder, penciled eye brows, eye liner, blue eye-shadow, blush, and melon-colored lipstick. Mary Kay would have been proud. When I arrived for breakfast, surrounded by companions with clean-washed faces and hints of pale lipstick, I felt I had a clown's face. A new-found freedom was born when I zipped my American face inside its carrying case. It would remain there until I prepared to board the plane back to Alaska, and even then I would apply it with a lighter hand.

Approximately ten people were in Elisabeth's room, not all of them staff. The only ones seated were Elisabeth and a woman I didn't know. The way they sat, bent forward with knees almost touching, hands resting atop a small wooden table, brought back an image of Betty and me moving the crystal ashtray on the Ouija Board in my pre-Angel days.

Broken chocolate bars lay on a center table, so I took a small piece before I moved over to stand near Gisele. She smiled and indicated silence with index finger across puckered lips. When the chocolate melted on my tongue, I discovered that not all chocolate was milk chocolate, and I longed for a place to spit. Fine European chocolate was wasted on my coarse palate.

A scraping sound came from the small table, and the gathering sighed as one. Gisele whispered that recently Elisabeth had discovered she could question the table and it would tap an answer. Oh great, just what I needed, more hocus pocus.

"Aren't we going to have a staff meeting?" I asked.

"No. She'll be table-tapping until bedtime."

"Is it okay if I go to bed?"

"She won't even know you're gone," Gisele assured me.

I stopped off at the loo to rinse the bitter chocolate from my mouth. Though thankful Elisabeth was table-tapping instead of asking me to Angel-write, I was disappointed in her using antiquated séance methods much ridiculed by modern thinking. Had I been misled by my infatuation? I knew that her interest in channeling spirit guides and her statements like "Death does not exist" caused many to be skeptical about her. Were those people right? Was she a charlatan? Were her methods invalid?

I'd traveled here at great expense to continue learning from this world-renowned doctor, but so far all I'd acquired was a dislike for dark chocolate.

*

I was late. I'd overslept then got lost between my cell and the dining room. Thank God for my new non-clown look; avoiding make-up shaved twenty minutes from my morning toilette. I was a bit winded when I speed-walked into the elegant dining hall. Sunlight streamed through stained glass windows, warming yards of polished wood. The silver gleamed and the glassware sparkled. I felt I'd stepped onto a movie set, for surely this was too rich to be everyday life. Behind the serving line, smiling black-robed women added to the feeling of fantasy.

My hunger, however, was real. I loaded a tray with scrambled eggs, bacon, cold toast, orange juice, and an apple to eat on break. Because I couldn't identify them or decide how they were to be eaten, I avoided all other choices, although they looked interesting. Tiny fish? Cooked whole tomatoes? No time for experimentation this morning; I had an important job to do. After all, I was Staff.

Last night at dinner, I'd discovered that participants who couldn't squeeze in at Elisabeth's table considered staff members the second most desired dining companions. We were celebrities of a sort. This morning I had no time for people's questions and stories. I needed to eat. I walked the length of the room and took a seat at an empty table crosswise from the others.

Halfway through my eggs, a nun joined me; she could have been the one I'd met yesterday but I wasn't sure. I did know that one nun was exceptionally tall, another came to my shoulder, another was very fat, and one looked like she could have helped God roll back the gravestone. Other than those four, all the other nuns, behind their serene smiles, looked alike inside their black habits.

Silently, other nuns joined us. They seemed to glide across the floor, flutter and settle at the table rather than sit, reminding me of ravens hunkering down to feast on road kill. But these birds were not eating. Several minutes passed before a thin priest with pinched brows took the seat at the head of the table. He and the nuns bowed heads, and I heard, "Our Father, bless . . ."

I stopped chewing and looked first at the priest then surveyed the room. Only then did I notice that the table where I sat was on a raised platform with a spindled railing that separated it from the room at large. Red-faced, I grabbed my plate, made apologies and rose to leave. In a chorus, they urged me to sit and finish my meal. It seems even nuns were curious. They plied me with questions about the mattresses placed in rooms not meant for sleeping.

I swallowed my last bite and made a hasty exit, wondering what happened to those infuriating Angels. According to their self-proclaimed job description, they were to protect, direct and educate me. (By now, I suspected that everyone has a set of Angels and all it takes to activate them is to ask them to take charge, though I didn't always succeed in activating mine.) If we were at home, they'd be chattering, Go here, Do this, Do that, Angels are love. It would've been helpful this morning if they'd mentioned, Not that table. It's reserved for clergy.

I hadn't heard a word from them since they whispered taxi in my ear at Heathrow. Granted, that was most helpful. Since then, it seemed they'd been neglecting me. Without a word of warning, they'd let me do one foolish thing after another. If this was the free will they preached about, I didn't much care for it.

CHAPTER EIGHTEEN
The Rose Garden

THE MORNING SESSION began with the cheery camp songs I hated, but I knew they worked to focus the participants and ready them to move into feelings. Gisele, Stephen, Bernard, and I sat with Elisabeth at the front of the room. A mattress, covered with a clean white sheet like an altar readied for sacrifice, lay on the floor between us and the others.

I was both nervous and excited. Today I'd prove myself; I'd function as a full-fledged staff member. Beside Gisele, Stephen, and Bernard, I'd watch participants for signs that they were "ready to process personal work," as Elisabeth put it. I'd tap them on the shoulder, receive a nod and lead them into a small room away from where Elisabeth was working in the main room. Once there I'd guide him/her to the root of their unfinished business and assist them to unburden themselves. I was itching to get started. After the close of this workshop, I'd be able to call myself a trained Facilitator with Shanti Nilaya.

As always, Elisabeth opened with stories. This time they weren't about her beloved cancer patients, or of treatments or hospital stays or utilizing the time between diagnosis and death to heal wounds of the soul. On this September morning, sitting in a pool of light streaming through windows that depicted a gentle Jesus, she served up Holocaust death.

We staff and participants walked with a twenty-year-old Elisabeth through the gates at Majdanek. We looked inside an abandoned railroad car half-full of adult and children's shoes and were repelled by the realization that the next car's floor was covered in human hair.

Elisabeth's voice swelled with compassion. She described the names, initials, messages—and drawings of butterflies—scratched into the walls and beams of the barracks where the condemned had slept five across on shelf-like beds in tiers from floor to ceiling. The butterflies, she said, "Spoke not of despair, but of freedom."

I felt, as the Brits say, "gob-smacked." Although I had read of Elisabeth's trek to Poland and her work with the International Voluntary Service for Peace in the days immediately following the end of WWII, the books didn't have the same impact as hearing her tell those events in her unique style. Her voice penetrated deep inside me and expanded my understanding. It allowed me to experience her words on a visceral level, as if I shared her experience firsthand.

If not for WWII, would Elisabeth have left her beloved Switzerland to become an expert on death and dying? The war was a major influence on her, from the age of thirteen, when Germany first invaded Poland. Aware of the suffering in Poland, she left home to volunteer. As a teenager she volunteered to help refugees. Postwar, she volunteered with Service for Peace and worked in Italy, France, and Poland to rebuild towns. She was only nineteen and came close to dying before she returned home. It was then she decided to become a doctor. Her passion was to relieve suffering. Was she given a future calling by her tormented culture, or had she been born with a destiny to fulfill?

Seated beside Elisabeth, I watched the entire assembly appear to dissolve. A gray-haired gentleman with a bulldog face bent forward, elbows on knees, and grasped his head in both hands. A number of men and women sat stoic and let tears drip unnoticed from their chins. Heads sank into shoulders, arms crossed chests as if to keep hearts from bursting. Some faces paled while others blazed red with white circles around eyes and mouth. I'd never before witnessed such an instant and all-inclusive response of pain in any audience.

This puzzled me. I'd seen Elisabeth's stories move audiences, but never before so intensely. A few usually remained aloof. Not so on this morning.

Then I remembered where I was. WWII was more than a distant historical event to these people. For them, WWII had happened in this very city, and across the Channel. To a little girl in the US, WWII was Mom at the kitchen table counting gas coupons before she decided if we would visit my grandparents for Thanksgiving. It was Uncle Daniel, home from the Army, playing Santa Claus. It was the game of Black-Out when air raid sirens sounded. It was car horns blasting, church bells ringing and us kids banging pie plates in the front yard and screaming, "The war's over. The war's over"—except for little sister Glenda, who got it wrong and yelled, "More soap. More soap." Mom said that was true too, since rationing would end and there would indeed be more soap.

In response to Elisabeth's invitation, a grandfatherly man kicked off his shoes and crawled onto the mat. His non-descript clothes and light coloring blended into the sheet. I knew he was on the mat, but the light played a trick and I swear I looked right through him.

"What do you have to tell us?" Elisabeth asked.

"I was only seventeen. I didn't know. I didn't know," he sobbed.

"What didn't you know?"

"Now they say he was a mad-man. A monster. But then he was Der Führer."

"And . . ." Elisabeth prompted.

"Now I am hated. People blame me for things I not do. I wear the uniform, yes. But I not kill all their families. I not even there. I was good soldier. I am good citizen." His body shook with his sobs. The eyes of other participants were on his every move. Some looked fearful, others angry. "Lies. Lies. They tell lies about me in my village." Elisabeth handed him the red hose and he moved from tears to violence.

After his rage was spent, Elisabeth ended the session with this declaration: "Given the right circumstances, within each individual resides both a Mother Teresa and a Hitler."

A woman in the front row gasped and covered her mouth.

Elisabeth announced the break, rose and left the room. To avoid another interrogation about the Angels, I left by a different door.

Gisele and I were in the courtyard smoking when Bernard rushed out of the meeting room and summoned me. "Come quick. Elisabeth wants you." What now, I wondered? Not more Angel nonsense I hoped.

I found her in the rose garden with a stocky woman. Without preamble, Elisabeth took me by the upper arm and pushed me back in the direction from which I'd come.

"You must stay with Rose," she whispered, gesturing to the woman in the garden. "Keep her out of main room. Do not put her on mat. She is very, very vulnerable. Under no circumstances put her on mat. Do you understand?"

What? I wasn't going to mat participants? It was as I suspected: the only reason I'd been invited to England was to Angel-write. My dream of a career other than addictions counselor took flight like white doves released at weddings. I'm sure my face betrayed my disappointment but Elisabeth seemed not to notice. "Okay," I agreed. What else was I to say? No one told Elisabeth no. It was her show. She was the boss.

Elisabeth introduced me to Rose in complimentary terms, hinting that I had unusual and exemplary skills. This confused me. Had she told this woman about the Angels? What else could she be referring to? To my knowledge,

Elisabeth hadn't observed me in any role other than Angel-messenger. Rose and I were to check in with Elisabeth at the noon break, but until then I was not to leave Rose's side.

Crap! I was shackled to this person for the rest of the morning and had no idea what I was to do. Rose stood among the rose bushes in a black dress with saucer-sized pink roses blooming all over it. No costume designer could have created two more opposite figures than Rose and me: she was a matronly fire-plug of a woman in proper Sunday-go-to-meeting dress complete with nylons and high heels. I was in jeans and a red t-shirt on which was printed, "You're not okay. I'm not okay. That's okay."

We took each other's measure. Then she started to talk in such heavily accented English that I could hardly understand her. This was going to be a very long morning.

Just listen, advised the Angels, arriving at last.

"Why I become so upset?" cried Rose. "None of my family went to the ovens. We are respected German citizens." Her English was guttural.

"Do you mind if I smoke?" I might as well make use of the time. Listen, smoke, and let Rose rattle on.

"Elisabeth worried because I have health condition. Doctors not find cause. Sometime I faint for no reason. Sometime I get nervous. I fall over."

"Hmm...and the doctors can't find the cause?"

"My husband pay specialists from all over, but no good. He love me very much, my husband. He worry. I go nowhere alone. What happen if I get upset and fall and hit head? He never forgive himself." She stopped talking to breathe in the fragrance of a large salmon-colored rose.

"Is your husband here with you?"

"No. I put my foot down. I tell him I do this alone. I tell him Dr. Ross not let anything bad happen to me. My father died three years ago. I not get over it. My husband, he not understand. He say, 'It's been three years, parents die.' This stress is taking my health. Last week, on street, I faint. No reason."

We left the rose garden, and in a roundabout way she took us toward the abbey's side entrance. "Did you hurt yourself when you fell?"

"A bruise, here." She touched her elbow. "My father and I closer than other fathers and daughters. The only time I relax is with my father. Now he is gone. I'm scared all the time. I was safe with my father. He love me very much."

"And you loved him." We'd entered the Abbey; she led and I followed. Where was she taking us? She seemed unfamiliar with the surroundings yet seemed to know where she was headed.

"Father not want us to marry, my husband and I. That is why husband glad father passed. He jealous of my father. Twenty-five years married and all the time he jealous." Her voice had become monotone. Abruptly she turned to the right, opened a door and stepped into an octagon-shaped room with windows on all sides. In the center of the floor was a mattress.

"I don't think we should be in here," I said.

"I just look around."

"Elisabeth told me you're not to work on the mat."

"We just sit a little while. I tired walking around, and this room, it is pleasant." Without waiting for me to agree or disagree, she sat on the edge of the mat and kicked off her shoes. Okay, I thought, what harm can come if we just sit on it?

"I want to hit the books one time. That okay?"

"Elisabeth said no, that you were to calm yourself."

Whack. "There. That is for the man in the room. He is cry-baby. Soldiers had privileges we civilians not have. . .Food" Whack! "Shoes" Whack! "Warm coats."

"Stop, you mustn't do this. Elisabeth said ..." It was no use; she didn't hear me. She was in feeling, and that feeling was anger. She was very, very angry. I was helpless to do anything other than manage the phone books and make sure she didn't hit me or hurt herself. Within a few minutes she was on her back on the mat, kicking and flailing like a two-year-old in mid-tantrum.

I was scared and didn't know what to do. I couldn't leave her. If I called for help, no one could hear me, and if someone did, it would just sound like someone screaming on a mat under the watchful eye of a trained facilitator. If I started screaming, I'd scare her. To make things worse, she'd given up on English and was speaking in what I assumed to be German.

I tried to comfort myself with the fact that I could do CPR if necessary. She continued her tantrum for perhaps fifteen minutes. Her rant stopped as abruptly as it began. She sat up, smoothed her dress over her knees and, to my relief, began speaking in English. "Did you see him?" she asked.

"Who?"

"My father. He come, give me permission to remember. He say, 'You can remember now. You are safe.' And I remember. I am six-years-old and we move to different house in different village. My father tell me I have to forget we are Jews. We are now German. To be Jew is to die. To be German is to live. He tell me our new name. Tell me I am never to say my real name—ever. I am very frightened. I not want to die. I not want my father and mother to die.

"My father was fine tailor and work for the officers of the local Gestapo in our new village. Officers come to house to be measured and pick up the clothes my father sew for them. Always I am polite and smile. They bring me candy. They like my blonde curls and blue eyes." Her hand smoothed her short, gray hair, and in that movement I could see the pretty child she must have been.

"One officer took special liking to our family and came to dinner every week. He bring sausages, butter and sugar. We eat good on those nights. Before he arrive, father coach me to smile and always say yes to the officer. I did not like him. He scare me. After our meal he always take me for walk. I obey my father and act happy. I tell officer how handsome he look in his uniform. We always go same place."

She pulled a tissue from the box beside her and blew her nose. "He put me on his shoulders and we walk on the path by the river. There he boast about the many dirty-Jew-children he drown in river. He tell me how they scream for help. He tell me how their faces look. He laugh. I remember my friend Berta who no longer come to school. I wonder if she is one of the children drowned. I hate him. I laugh with him so he not throw me in the river. What I do, Jan? I am Jew. Not German as my husband believes."

No words came to me. How was I to help this woman? Again the Angels advised just listen, and I did.

"Now I remember about when I faint on street. A hand touch my shoulder and I turn around to see who it is. It is a Rabbi. I faint." She continued, "We be married twenty-five years and I am still virgin. I tell husband my body too small for sex. I tell him doctors say no sex. But is because I not want him to touch me. He know this before we marry. I not lie to him. He love me very much, my husband."

I'm sure my mouth dropped open; a marriage without sex was incomprehensible to me. I was from the school that believed sex was the cure for most marital problems, and I wondered how one managed in a sexless marriage. Why get married at all if not because of sex? More mysterious was that Rose said her marriage was a happy one.

"We go now," she said. She stood up, slipped into her high heels and prepared to go as if nothing more had happened than conversation between two friends. "You change my life, Jan. I tell Elisabeth you help me find out who I am. No more lies."

I wanted to plead with her to say nothing; surely, this would mean I'd be sent away in disgrace for disobeying a direct order from Elisabeth. But Rose said she decided secrets had caused her nervous fainting and that health for her meant truth in all matters.

I dared not ask her to betray herself on my account. And, besides, I feared for her. What was to happen to her marriage to a German man when he discovered his wife was a Jew? Would old hatreds still control his heart? Would they both remain content in a sexless marriage? What would happen to her social standing when it became known her family had passed as German when others had died because they would or could not pass? I'd heard enough in the main room to know the prejudice against Jews who denied their heritage to escape persecution.

It seemed to me that Rose saw her future bathed in freedom—freedom from hiding and freedom to discover who she was, a new beginning, a total disruption of her life as she had lived it for fifty years. Had I been witness to her liberation or her distruction?

That mat session or, more accurately, Rose's story, marked my entry into a lifelong reverence for the complexity of the human experience. I'd studied Jung and was familiar with the unconscious, but this was my first glimpse of the power of what we do not know—how what we have forgotten, or perhaps have never known, can shape and control our lives or even dictate who we are.

I was frightened for Rose.

CHAPTER NINETEEN
Violin Music

DURING THE REMAINING three days at the abbey, I functioned as an official Shanti Nilaya facilitator. That week, working under the watchful eyes of Elisabeth, ended my trainee status. I'd achieved my goal. Before the week ended, I expected to be questioned by Elisabeth and perhaps other staff, reminded of my obligation to continue my personal work, have a file opened to record my hours of training and supervision, and receive a certificate with my name and the date in fancy script. I'd have proof that I was fully qualified to be a facilitator at conferences or perhaps, someday, be full time in Elisabeth's Foundation.

No acknowledgement of this sort occurred. Sometime during the week, I'd been awarded qualified-facilitator status without my knowledge. No one said, "Congratulations! Welcome aboard." Not even Elisabeth.

I learned that although the Foundation required attendance at three conferences to qualify as a facilitator, Elisabeth didn't bother with credentials, courses of study or supervision hours. She wasn't impressed with degrees, theories learned, tests passed. She believed in deep personal healing and psychological health; for her, the only road to that health was to complete one's unfinished business.

Halfway through day three, I bumped into a bit of my own unfinished business. For two and a half days, I'd listened to horror stories from Nazi SS Guards and Camp survivors. I'd heard adults who, as children, were forced into hiding when the German army marched into their villages and executed families and friends. I'd learned that after the surrender German citizens suffered from lack of food, fuel, and medicines, and that their women and girls were raped by Russian soldiers.

During the retelling of these atrocities, I'd stayed present. Although empathetic, I was able to remain outside their experience. I prodded, pushed, and supported these individuals to look at their pains of the past and examine how current-day difficulties might be rooted in these past traumas.

Then a well-dressed English woman—thin, beautiful, perfectly groomed and dripping diamonds, emeralds, and gold—rendered me inadequate and in pain. For safety reasons I made her remove her jewelry before beginning mat work. As she placed each ring, bracelet, and pendant into my hand, she told how it had come into her possession: birthday gift, anniversary gift, or just-because-the-sun-is-shining gift. All from her loving husband. What could be her hidden burden? Guilt over affairs? Infertility? Death of child or parent? Perhaps it would be the diagnosis of stage-four cancer. If it wasn't unresolved bereavement or impending disease, what pain could this picture of ease and privilege possibly carry?

Without prompting, she removed her shoes, climbed onto the mat and grabbed the hose. The quick onset of her fury startled me. Bam. Bam. Bam. Phone book pages flew around the room. Soon the mat and surrounding floor were covered with debris. Pages clung to the hose and flew over her head. No sounds in the room except bam, bam, bam. Soon she and I were hip-deep in paper. Her strength and endurance spoke of hours at the gym.

"Use your words," I coached.

"How dare you!" she screamed. "Bloody tyrant." Bam. Bam. Bam.

She scolded a husband who met her every need, want or wish. She cursed him for doting on her and spending time with their two healthy children. He prized her parents and saw her siblings as gifts. The anger, it seemed, was because she thought it was his fault she had done nothing of value with her life. She whined that his adoration had stifled her.

My palms itched to grab the hose from her manicured fingers and beat some sense into her pretty blonde head. She continued to scream and destroy books. All I could do was stay out of her way and stack more phonebooks within reach. Beyond these mechanics of externalization, I was useless.

However, her work stirred something in my psyche; Tears pressed behind my eyes. Breathing was difficult. I couldn't think clearly. My hands trembled. Elisabeth would name my response "unfinished business."

I managed to control myself until Ms. Pampered left the room, but barely. I was in trouble.

A mat session would put me back together in short order, but I needed a facilitator. My first thoughts were to protect my status: Maintain your professional persona; don't show your vulnerability; you'll be denied facilitator status if you ask for help; as a professional you should be past all this. Drawing on my two-plus years of self-discovery, I recognized these thoughts as defense mechanisms, lies that would keep me stuck and in pain.

After our session that morning, staff was informed Elisabeth had flown at dawn to Germany to make a house-call on a child dying of cancer. She would be back in the afternoon. Elisabeth off campus meant no staff meeting. We were on our own.

I sat with Gisele at lunch. One look into my face and she asked, "Are you all right?"

"I need help." After lunch, we found an empty room. I took my place on the mat. Gone was my facade of professionalism, gone any pretense of control. I wanted relief.

Trust, and experience with the process, allowed me to put my defenses aside and concentrate on feelings. Expertly, Gisele guided me from my irrational anger toward Ms. Pampered with the perfect husband to my grief over two failed marriages. Exposed was my unfulfilled desire to be cherished. With Gisele's help, I discovered that my head and heart were in conflict. In my heart, I longed to be taken care of. I desired intimacy. But

my head told me, "I have to take care of myself."
This attitude prevented others from getting close,
especially men. That realization was a bitter
pill. Even as a child, I'd prided myself on being
independent. Yet the years I'd spent in an abusive
marriage, cowering and sacrificing my sense of self
while trying to appease my alcoholic and violent
husband, I'd lost my early feistiness and hated
myself for doing so. Dependence was weakness.
Dependent women made me cringe. I'd never
again be one of them. I saw how I'd put myself in
conflict and found relief in that understanding.

Only after returning home, and letting
myself relax into a shared relationship with
Jerry, would I come to understand the concept
of healthy interdependency.

The session ended in laughter. Gone was the
need to cry. Energy and focus returned. I felt a
twinge of regret that I'd not been able to move Ms.
Pampered beyond her anger to discover what may
lay hidden beneath. Through the remainder of the
week, I watched Ms. Pampered for any signs that
she wasn't functioning and saw none. I dismissed
my regret on the basis that I'd done no harm.

Several weeks after I returned home, a
letter arrived, forwarded from Shanti Nilaya
headquarters. It was from Ms. Pampered. The
envelope sat on my desk for three days before

I had the courage to open it. In her careful handwriting: "You cured me of my life-long anxiety disorder. I'm off medication and doing well. I can never thank you enough." I laughed out loud. Proof again that I can't know what another's experience of me is, on or off the mat.

*

By day four, I'd memorized the route from bedroom to loo to dining room and was comfortable with the new foods I found there—kippers for breakfast? bangers? There were no more table-tapping sessions and no more requests for "yellow pages." The arc of an LDT was such that by the fourth day participants were clearly divided between those who'd been on the mats and those who hadn't. Two of the had-nots were an elderly couple.

I'd been on the abbey steps when they arrived. Small and bent, the gentleman held the wife's elbow as they climbed stairs. She used a cane and spoke roughly in a language I didn't recognize. When they reached the top and started toward the door, the woman shook his hand away, turned and whacked him with her cane. The blow landed across his chest with enough force that he took two steps back. He nodded, bowed his head, and followed her through the door.

Daily I watched her smack, whack and poke him with that cane. He remained calm, never left her side and behaved pleasantly. They always ate at Elisabeth's table and conversed in German. I wondered why Elisabeth allowed the abuse to continue even in her presence.

Through another staffer, I learned parts of their story. The husband was a concert violinist who hadn't touched his violin in the six years since their daughter's funeral. She'd been only twenty, with a promising career ahead of her, when she was murdered. She was beaten, then stabbed, and finally her throat was slashed. Both parents had warned the daughter her boyfriend was dangerous; other women had complained of his violence. She wouldn't listen. After her death, police questioned the boyfriend, but he wasn't charged. No one had been arrested for the daughter's murder.

During breakfast of day four, with no change in the wife's behavior, I wondered if either of them would benefit from attending the LDT. I was sure they would leave as miserable as they had arrived.

*

The work of the LDT closed Thursday at the lunch break. Elisabeth instructed the participants to use the afternoon to prepare a celebration for that evening as a thank you to the staff. More importantly, the party was to provide a time for people to share what burden they were leaving behind and what they were taking home from their workshop experience.

For me, Thursday evening celebrations were always magical. Just four days before, when the participants first met, they were strangers. Because arrangements to attend were made weeks or months in advance, participants had had ample time to stew over their private reasons for coming. They arrived tired, out of their element and embroiled in painful memories. Postures were rigid, arms crossed over chests, eye contact avoided. Then, as if by alchemy, at the closing celebration they would dance, sing and embrace one another. During these occasions, Elisabeth became childlike, enthusiastic, willing to be surprised. Gone was her "Death and Dying Lady" persona. She was no longer the great healer and became a very small woman in wrinkled clothes and bad hair who radiated joy.

In mid-afternoon on this Thursday, staff discovered that one of the participants was absent: the elderly husband of the cane-wielding wife. After a thorough search by abbey and LDT staff, it was determined he was nowhere on the grounds. Rumors flew, but no one knew his whereabouts. Reluctantly the search was abandoned. His wife refused to notify authorities. "What they do? They do nothing," she said.

During the evening activities, the door opened and in strolled the elderly man, carrying a violin case. After a bow and apology to Elisabeth, he walked to the front of the room, opened the case and after some plunking, began to play his violin. His wife sat silent as tears washed her face, the first she'd cried since the funeral, we were told.

Gisele told me Elisabeth had facilitated the couple while I was busy in one of the smaller rooms. I'd already made up a story in my head about their daughter's murder, why he no longer played the violin and why he put up with his wife's abuse. It went something like this: she blamed him because he didn't save their daughter; he accepted her abuse because he felt guilty. I was wrong!

He'd refused to play the violin because it was through the violin that he and his daughter had been most intimate. Her love of the violin was so great, he felt it wrong to play when the daughter could not. He'd failed her. Therefore, he declared himself unworthy to play.

The wife was angry with him for being selfish and felt he hurt her intentionally by refusing to play. For her, his music brought pleasant memories; she could close her eyes and imagine her daughter in the room. Each time she refused to play his violin he felt as if he killed their daughter again.

I was sorry I'd missed seeing Elisabeth facilitate this reconciliation, but it served to remind me to let the individual on the mat direct the process. Only they knew where the scars were. Only they knew what needed to be said. Our job as facilitators was to walk beside the individual as witness and to listen carefully enough to know when they strayed off course.

While the gentle man played, a nun passed me a note. I had a phone call. An emergency. Immediately I thought of my children back in Alaska. The only person who knew how to contact me was Jerry, who was monitoring Christine and Travis. What could possibly justify a transatlantic phone call?

Once I got to the phone, Jerry was quick to explain it didn't concern the kids. He'd received word his mother was hospitalized in Seattle and not expected to live. He needed to go to her. Jeff, always faithfully there, would watch Christine and Travis. Relief flooded me; my kids were safe.

He went on, "I guess this is the reason I couldn't vacation with you in England. I didn't understand at the time."

I'd been so very angry with Jerry because he refused to join me just because it didn't feel right. Now it seemed that, practical as he was, he too was subject to, if not Angels, at least to premonitions.

The Angels whispered, *He's the one.*

Too shaken to return to the party, I went to my room. Gisele found me there, and I told her about the call. Then she asked if I wanted to co-facilitate an LDT in Germany the following week. "I need a second person and we work well together," she said.

With only a moment's thought I said, "Yes!" Oh boy, Oh boy. I get to see Germany plus get paid for it. What a wonderful surprise.

Friday morning, as Gisele and I headed out the abbey door on our way to Heathrow, I had a thought. "The LDT will be conducted in English, right?"

She stopped short. "No. Don't you speak German? French?"

I shook my head no.

We hugged, promised to stay in touch, and said good-bye.

CHAPTER TWENTY
Dried Apples and a Crone

MY TIME IN ENGLAND finished, Elisabeth and staff arrived at Heathrow driven by generous volunteers who also helped carry our luggage inside. These were the same volunteers who'd organized the housing, the food, and met my every need—out of love for Elisabeth and belief in her work.

There were seven of us staff from vastly different locations—Germany, Sweden, Australia, California, New York, and Alaska. We were saying good-byes, sorting luggage and checking our passports and tickets when Bernard looked around and asked, "Where's Elisabeth?" Like a herd of sheep responding to a dog's bark, our heads came up, eyes alert, and rotated 180 degrees.

Approaching at three o'clock was Elisabeth with an elderly couple. "What now?" breathed Paul, a veteran of travels with Elisabeth. They looked to be the British counterpart of a homeless couple on any street corner in America. All that was lacking was a sign declaring "family on hard times" or "will work for food."

Both had dried-apple faces, brown and wizened evidence of lives lived long and hard. I longed for my camera, but it was packed. They reminded me of faces I'd seen looking out from pages of *National Geographic*. With rounded shoulders and dressed in brown monochromatic clothes and worn-out shoes, they stood squished together as if blended into one individual with two heads. In their posture, I read a lifetime of mutual struggle met with acceptance and strength.

Not wanting to be asked for more than I could give, whether money or caring, I kept my distance. While others rushed forward to help sort out whatever situation had arisen, I continued to fuss with my luggage.

Elisabeth and the couple looked like a committee of little people coming to wish us well. They moved with the familiarity of individuals who had spent time together or were related.

It was as if Elisabeth took on their appearance and attitudes. Later I came to understand that Elisabeth's ability to connect immediately with strangers was due to her being totally present.

Elisabeth explained, "They lost their luggage. Their tickets are gone. They're stranded." I wasn't alone in my disbelief. She'd been completely taken in by this obvious con! I watched Paul question the couple and ask Elisabeth what action she wanted taken. When it became evident she was going to buy them tickets, over the objections of the couple, who were bargaining for cash, I had to step away.

From a distance, I watched as Elisabeth seemed not to understand they wanted cash and directed Paul to use her credit card to buy them airline tickets. Adhering to one of her cardinal rules, "Take care of the physical body first," she sent Bernard to buy sandwiches and tea for the couple. Then she produced a chocolate bar, seemingly from thin air, and forced it on the couple saying, "Eat, Eat."

To my chagrin, because my plane was the last to depart, she instructed me to keep the couple company. As we sat on hard benches, lined up like crows on a fence, I wondered what other passengers thought about our odd threesome—a fortyish, frizz-haired blonde American and these two miniature derelicts. Conversation was impossible since I spoke only English and they spoke something else. I would have been content to gaze into near space and construct fantasy photographs from the sights around me, but I was not afforded that luxury. The woman wanted to talk.

She touched my hand to get my attention, and in broken English and gestures, we communicated. I was humbled by their knowledge of more than their native language, especially due to their seemingly reduced circumstances, and I was thoroughly shamed to realize my prior judgment had been wrong. I'd concocted a story to fit a situation I didn't understand. Since I didn't speak their language and hadn't known what was being said, I'd jumped to conclusions based on my cultural bias.

Their story, like a print in the developer tray, came into focus slowly. First, the blacks in the photo emerged: they were making their yearly pilgrimage to their son's grave; he had been killed in the war. Now all the lighter shades slowly emerged: although their money and tickets had been stolen, they were not without means. The objections this couple made to Elisabeth was over her buying their tickets. They were willing to wait in the airport two more days; they'd already been waiting while their daughter made the arrangements necessary to replace the stolen tickets. They'd asked only to borrow enough cash for food to sustain them while they waited. They didn't want or need Elizabeth to buy their tickets. They were proud, independent folk caught in temporary circumstances beyond their control. Once Elisabeth agreed to accept repayment for the tickets, they accepted her generosity.

The incident taught me a lesson about culture and my limited view of the world. It also further muddled my efforts to capture Elisabeth inside a frame so I could say, "Yes, that's Elisabeth Kübler-Ross." She continually complained she was broke, going to starve for sure, couldn't pay salaries or traveling expenses. Then, when presented with strangers in need, Elisabeth spent money as if it were limitless. A phone call arrived from the parent of a dying child and she boarded a plane to make a house call, always at her own expense. Terminally ill patients and bereaved families attended her week-long workshops at no charge. As members of her organization, we were required to provide services for the terminally ill for free, even in our private practices. It is my belief that no person who applied for a scholarship was ever turned away. Yet Elisabeth's basic character was that of a thrifty Swiss, her description of herself.

*

On the twelve-hour flight home, I had time to digest my time in rural England and Scotland. (I'd visited them even though Jerry hadn't joined me as we'd planned.) Because I had taken as my own the Brits' practice of public privacy (no eye contact, no obligation to engage strangers), I didn't converse with my seat companion on my return trip. What a month earlier would have seemed rude, was now liberating. I'd heard enough life stories in the last few weeks.

Unlike my feelings on the flight to London, I did not expect to die on this journey home. On the way to the London conference, I'd been unable to envision a life beyond achieving my greatest dream. Now my mind was filled with plans to make use of my official status as a facilitator in mat-work—externalization therapy. There would be life after London!

I wondered how my children were doing. A month is a long time to be away from family. Jeff would pick me up from the airport because Jerry was still in Seattle with his mother. She'd rallied after he arrived and was expected to go home soon.

I listened to the hum of the jet engines and remembered with fondness the volunteers who had taken me into their homes, showered me with English hospitality and tea and answered my intrusive questions with good humor. I'd asked one hostess, "How do I not act like a rude American? What do we do that is so rude?"

She answered that we talk too loud in public and share our opinions when they are neither solicited nor wanted. Why do we Americans think everyone within earshot is interested in what we think? In short, Americans are full of themselves.

Near the end of my stay I'd observed this behavior myself and was embarrassed by it. When American college students boarded the train to Edinburgh—with no attention to other passengers—they filled the coach with boisterous chatter and laughter so loud it made normal conversation impossible. Since Europeans aren't accustomed to screaming at one another, the students' actions silenced everyone. In retrospect, I see the difference in cultures as a matter of age and travel experiences. Our young culture is stuck in the junior-high stage, and we're used to the luxury of our own plentiful space. Most of us live our whole lives within our own borders. Europeans seem more mature, perhaps because they cross into other countries frequently.

No loud Americans on this flight home, though.

My seat companion read. I listened to the engines and remembered an unsettling incident in Britain that recently changed my understanding of what it means to be an alcoholic. It's always been easy for me to empathize with families and associates of the addicted, but empathy for the addict? Not so much. It took a haughty Brit and a crone to help me see things from the addict's point of view.

During my travels after the conference, I'd taken the tour I'd planned, even though Jerry couldn't be with me. I'd been on a bus to Glastonbury, in Somerset, sitting next to an odorous old woman. She appeared to be wearing her complete wardrobe: a skirt over trousers, shirts (more than one) under a sweater topped with a long black coat. I'd first met her while waiting to board the bus in Bath, and she'd asked me to watch her bundles for "just a minute," which stretched to thirty-five and denied me a bathroom opportunity. When the bus driver tried to stow these same bags in the luggage compartment the woman caused a fuss; she grabbed them, sat by the window and stuffed them under her seat where she checked on them continually.

At the first stop out of Bath, a well-dressed woman boarded. Because all other seats were occupied, she was forced to sit with the crone and me. I moved to the center seat and the new arrival sat on the aisle. When she sat down, a heavy object poked my hip.

"I'm the keeper of the abbey," she said and pulled back her gray jacket to show me the six-inch key that hung from a chain attached to her belt. (It seemed there were abbeys all over England.) Small of frame, she seemed to gain stature with the showing, as if the mere display of the key gave her an authority reserved for a select few.

"Cook and clean for the priests, do you?" asked the crone on my right.

"I hire cooks and maids for those jobs. Keeper is an administrative position," Ms. Abbey said, and she slipped the key into her skirt pocket as if it might be stolen.

"Such an unusual key. Does it actually lock the abbey doors?" I asked.

"Yes. . . yes. Why would you think otherwise?"

"It looks so old," I said.

"Old, yes. The abbey dates from the 16th century."

"And it's used? I mean lived in still?" The antiquity of Europe astounded me. In my world of Anchorage, Alaska, the oldest building standing was constructed in 1938.

"Yes. The Fathers live there, as do I and some staff. Parts of the abbey are open to the public a few hours a week. We have services on Sunday. We're part of the National Trust, you see." She sniffed and jutted her chin when speaking of public access. Her posture became very erect with eyes focused straight forward. I almost giggled at her obvious snobbery.

Just then, the crone said, "It'll be dark soon. He said we'd get in before dark."

"Is it important to get there before dark?" I asked.

"Got to," she said as she stared at out the window at the green countryside.

"Why's that?"

"So much to do."

"Are you being met?"

She chuckled. "Being met, me? No." She turned back to the window and her hand slipped down to touch a bundle as if to reassure herself all was in order. "Had a daughter but she's tired of her old Mum."

"How's that?" I asked, maintaining the rude-American role.

She didn't seem to mind. "I'm an alcoholic," she said. "I live in doorways and warehouses. It's dangerous for us women. They're those out to rob or rape." She displayed no embarrassment, just looked out the window and asked me the time. "Light's starting to fail. So much to do."

"What's to do?" Again me with the personal question.

She counted on her fingers. "First, find a bottle to ward off the sickness. Then find a safe place to sleep." Her hands dropped into her lap. "New town won't be easy. Last week I shared space with a mate and woke up with a bump on my head and no morning nip."

There went my illusion that those who lived on the streets were a large benevolent fraternity who looked out for one another. That made me sad.

We'd stopped to offload some passengers. Ms. Abbey dug into her large purse and brought out a tray of chocolate-covered mints. She offered me one. I passed them to the crone, who used a dirty index finger to dig two from the tray. Ms. Abbey let out a tiny startled sound, and I flushed. I'd over-stepped. I'd assumed generosity where there was none.

It was dusk by the time we reached the crone's stop. As she collected her bundles, I slipped her a five-pound note. She rewarded me with a smile. She was guaranteed her "morning nip." I swelled with righteous goodwill.

When the bus started to move again, Ms. Abbey snatched away my glow. "That was too much. It could put her in hospital, or worse, kill her."

Inwardly I'd struggled to justify my actions. How was I to know how much booze five pounds would buy?

The bus stopped, and when Ms. Abbey got off, I glimpsed a red brick wall in the distance and wondered if that was her abbey.

Thoughts returning to where I was, I twisted in my seat and decided to walk to the restroom to splash water on my face. It was distasteful to realize that I'd often played Ms. Abbey to my alcoholic clients when my role was to understand and help.

CHAPTER TWENTY-ONE

Whispers and Whales

OVER THE NEXT five or six years, Elisabeth often phoned me. "Come to London. I need you. No reliable people over here." It was hard to say no to those invitations, but I couldn't afford to accept. She didn't pay travel expenses and the Facilitator salary for one LDT wasn't enough to offset my costs. She hadn't even paid me for facilitating the first time in London when I'd graduated from trainee to official Facilitator. I continued to be the volunteer Alaska Coordinator, working with the terminally ill and their families, and I also organized and facilitated at workshops and intensive trainings for the Elisabeth Kübler-Ross Foundation.

Yet I still had to hold down my full-time job at the Mat-Su Council on Alcohol and Drug Abuse for three years after returning from London. There, my confidence grew and I acquired a following of clients, both individuals and groups.

When I left the Council, I opened a private practice. I treated individuals, lectured about home health, and organized and facilitated my own workshops for childhood sexual abuse survivors and rape victims. I held workshops on anger, grief, and bereavement. I also conducted critical incident debriefings for EMTs, firemen and law enforcement personnel.

Although I didn't use the hose and mat at every counseling session, Elisabeth's teachings were the foundation upon which I based all of my work. I believed her directive, "Do your own work before you can help others," as surely as I believed I needed oxygen.

Elisabeth continued to ask if I'd sent yellow pages. My answer was always no. A few times, after we hung up, I'd ask the Angels if they had anything for her. The messages they gave me were praise for her work, and they added that her spirit guides were pleased. The Angels always ended with the declaration "Angels are love." It felt phony, as if I was simply flattering Elisabeth, so I didn't see any purpose in sending those messages along.

After my return from Europe, the Angels began to fade. They were available if I called them forward for a stranger who showed up on my doorstep, but this seldom happened any more. Although the teen group still dropped by and talked about how the Angels worked in their lives, they no longer asked for writings. They visited much less after Jerry and I married and moved to Palmer, Alaska.

No longer did I take up the pen and wait for direction from the Angels. No longer did they speak in an alien voice. No more whispers in my left ear. Instead, I received insights that felt like guidance from a helpful entity that stayed out of the way. Our communication became internal.

Still, before counseling sessions, I'd always ask the Angels to be present. It wasn't that I prayed. It was more that I turned on my intuition, switched focus from broadcast to receive. I told myself, and anyone who would listen, that Angels don't exist, yet I invited them to every session or difficult situation. Startling insights about a client would frequently pop out of my mouth. The accuracy of these blurts shocked me, but with repeated validation, my confidence increased. I stopped questioning the source and claimed the insights as my own. No more could I say, "It's the Angels. It's not me."

Sometimes I reminded myself what professor Gregg Furth told me about the Angels being part of the Collective Unconscious. Perhaps they were evolving into being intuition instead of voices; perhaps the Angels were, after all, a part of my own psyche that I'd previously refused to assimilate.

That was all reasonable. Then my eyes would drift to the square crystal on my desk and I'd question that explanation. No part of my psyche could have known the story of the young mother who gave me the crystal as reward for "saving her life." Her children were kidnapped by a violent ex-husband. She contemplated suicide until the Angels assured her the children would be returned and after time in her care they would regain their health. Those words, written on my yellow legal pad, gave her the will to live. Months later, her children were returned as foretold by the writing.

Then there was Troy, burglarizing homes. The Angels gave him a severe scolding, not the action I'd have taken. And what about the carved ring returned to me at the first LDT though I'd lost it at home? The information that had spilled from my pen continued to mystify me.

So who were they? Where did they go? Why did they work through me? I would never understand.

*

Within a few years, the need for health insurance and retirement benefits prompted me to close my private practice and accept a position with the Palmer Police Department as a 911 operator. I certainly had the skills to deal with people in crisis who called for emergency help.

I used vacation time to continue my association with Elisabeth's Foundation—which by then had moved to West Virginia—and I planned my final LDT in January 1988, again at Meier's Lake Conference Center where I'd attended my first. In my role as Alaska Coordinator, I again rented the conference center, hired cooks, and advertised for participants. Excited to have a week away from 911 calls, I looked forward to spending time with Elisabeth and renewing friendships with other staff. Most of all, I wanted to re-experience life as a disciple of Elisabeth Kübler-Ross, seven years after we'd first crossed paths.

A week before the workshop, I glanced up from the 911 console and saw a small beige whale travel through the upper left quadrant of my vision. With it came an odd sensation that passed in seconds but left me feeling strange, out of context with my surroundings. I turned to my co-worker. "If I pass out, you need to know what just happened," and I told her about the whale.

I had no pain, no physical symptoms. I just felt that somehow the real me had been misplaced. Later that day I sensed I'd been permanently altered but didn't know how. No one around me—coworkers, family, supervisors—gave any indication that I was behaving differently. The old cliché "at sea" describes how I felt: at sea with no land in sight, nothing and no one to give me my bearings.

On the day of the LDT, I felt out of step. Events were moving too fast as I coordinated check-in, reconnected with staff members, set up the room and decided who would give the lectures on the five emotions and the four quadrants.

The opening activities sped by. I had trouble following what was being said at the staff meeting. I couldn't focus. I mixed up participants' names and stories. Years later, I'd retain the discomfort about a lecture but no memory of it. Did I lecture and do a terrible job? Or did I not give one?

Although no one indicated to me that I was less than normal, Elisabeth called me aside and assigned me the role of room monitor. She didn't want people in distress wandering off on their own. Elisabeth had a strict rule: no participant was to leave the room after the externalization process started, in case the stories, tears, and anger from the mat affected those who watched, connecting them to their own unfinished business. I felt hurt that after all my efforts in making the LDT happen, I wasn't going to facilitate.

The morning had barely started when a young amputee bolted for the door. During introductions, she'd spoken of the accident in which she lost her arm. One could see she was upset; her voice was strained and she looked ready to cry. At the door, I blocked her exit. A large woman, she pushed me aside and stormed out. In my confused state, I remained in the room when the proper action was to follow her outside, stay with her, and gently get her to verbalize. Her accident happened less than a year before, so it was important to move with caution so as not to re-traumatize her.

As staff, my most important role was to keep participants safe. By letting her leave alone, I'd put her at risk. Yet when another staffer followed her outside, I wondered why. I didn't understand my error.

At the break, Rita, an Alaska Native healer who was one of the attendees, pulled me aside. "I see you not well."

"I'm okay," I said, but the tears started. Rita led me into one of the private rooms and sat me on the mat.

"You be still," she instructed. "I'm a healer. I know when people not well. Lay down."

I was beyond objecting. She held her hands away from my body and moved them around. I felt heat radiating from them. It calmed me. After a few minutes, maybe fifteen, I felt able to take my place back in the main room.

Throughout the next four days, Rita caught me between sessions and ministered to me. There were no words, just her hands and deep breathing. If not for her and those mini-retreats, I feel sure I couldn't have completed the week. As it was, I avoided interacting with participants, spent much of my time in my cabin, and didn't speak at staff meetings. Now, when I travel back to that time, instead of thoughts or feelings in my head, I find black space shaped like the inside of my skull.

I'd been home several days when Jerry said, "You're not talking. What's going on?"

I searched my mind to see if I was angry or keeping a secret.

"Just re-entry syndrome," I said.

Several weeks after the LDT concluded, the small beige whale appeared again. I called a friend and co-facilitator. "What do you suppose is up with this little whale?"

"Maybe it's part of your totem," she offered.

"That's probably it. I've seen whales from my hospital bed at the birth of each of my children.

Don't suppose I'm pregnant, do you?" We both laughed and concluded I must be having a spiritual experience.

The most noticeable change in my behavior was the rage that hit suddenly and consumed me. These episodes were not healthy anger brought on by injustice; this rage burst out for no reason.

One night after dinner, Jerry and I had a couple of drinks and I fell into a rage again. I'm sure it made no sense. I grabbed car keys and screeched out of the driveway. It was dark, probably in February, though it might have been early March. Ice and snow were still on the roads.

I drove to Hatcher's Pass, up the same steep, twisty road I'd taken with Elisabeth the first time we met. Even in summer the road was dangerous. Because of my job with Palmer Police Department, I knew there were more auto fatalities recorded on it than any other place statewide.

How far up the mountain I traveled I don't know. I do know that on my drive down, singing at scream volume, I looked down at the speedometer. The needle sat at 100 mph. I thought that was the funniest number I'd ever seen on a car's dash.

When I reached the bottom of the mountain, I drove to a friend's house. She took me in, called Jerry and put me to bed. Did either of them scold me? I don't think so. Did the Angels save my life? Perhaps.

Another memory: it was a warm spring day in April or early May and I had errands to run. When I tried to leave the house, things became complicated. I walked to the car and discovered I didn't have keys. They must be on my desk. Retrieved keys and returned to the car. No purse. Returned to the house, picked up my purse. Returned to the car. No keys. I repeated this exercise numerous times, each time surprised to be missing an essential item. Finally, after much effort, I arrived at the car with keys, purse, and sunglasses.

I looked at my watch; an hour had passed. With no worry about my ability to drive, I went to my bank, verbally abused a teller, and then drove to Anchorage, fifty miles away. I managed to return home without incident or at least without damage to the car.

In May, the whale paid me another visit, same place, same lack of pain or other symptoms. I wondered if perhaps it wasn't a spiritual experience. Maybe the whale was an eye problem. I called my optometrist.

After a thorough eye exam, and without saying a word, the doctor left the room and returned with a stethoscope. He listened to the arteries in my neck, then left the room again. Still no explanation. I began to get scared. No eye doctor had ever used a stethoscope on me before. After what seemed a long time, he came back and handed me a paper with a name, address and time written on it.

I said, "You're going to tell me this isn't my eyes, right?"

He nodded. "This is the name of the best cardiovascular surgeon in the state. You have an appointment with him tomorrow morning. Go home and don't move your neck." That was the only instruction I received.

Because I was very upset, I walked outside, sat in my car and smoked two cigarettes. Later I learned that smoking was an even worse action than moving my neck. What was I to tell Jerry about the surgeon appointment? He'd ask why and I'd have to say, "I don't know."

Next day the surgeon explained to Jerry and me that there was a ninety-five percent blockage in my left carotid artery. My brain was starved for oxygen and had been for at least six months. The left carotid artery feeds the brain's left hemisphere where analytical, sequential, logical, objective and rational thought occurs, as well as language. The doctor explained that small chunks of plaque were breaking loose from the blockage and traveling to my brain.

I was having strokes. The small beige whale was a blood clot passing through the optical center. My brain was under siege.

The only treatment was surgery. He would remove the blockage then graft a vein from my leg into the artery to reduce the risk of recurrence. Possible outcomes: full recovery and return to normal function; or loss of speech; or loss of vison; or permanent brain damage. He made no mention that I might already have suffered brain damage due to oxygen deprivation.

Jerry and I agreed to surgery.

I felt confused but figured that surgery would put everything right. No anxiety. No fear.

On our drive home from Anchorage, Jerry was quiet. We'd driven about half way when I gathered enough courage to ask why he wasn't talking.

He said, "You're a visual person. You love photography. I'm just trying to figure out how I'm going to explain the world to you if you lose your sight."

I cried all the way home.

CHAPTER TWENTY-TWO
Melting Ice Cream

THE SUN SHONE and the day was glorious when I left the hospital. My spirits were high. The collar/bandage around my neck made it impossible to turn my head, but I didn't mind. The only discomfort was the surgery site on my left leg near the ankle where they'd harvested a vein for the graft.

Christine was home from college on summer break. Both Jerry and Christine acted as if they wanted to wrap me in cotton and put me to bed. I wasn't having any of that.

The second we got home, I spied a most amazing scene that had to be photographed.

Leota in the dandelions after surgery

I rushed to find camera, film, tripod; I had a photo-shoot to direct. Why all the excitement? Dandelions! Twenty-four hours of daylight with some rain had produced an amazing crop of dandelions. Jerry hadn't mowed because he'd spent his days at the hospital in Anchorage with me. Nothing would do but for him and Christine to kneel in all that yellow while I snapped shot after shot. Then I turned the camera over to them and knelt to be photographed.

The pictures turned out wonderful and I was glad to have them. When I looked at them a decade or so later, I filled with gratitude for the loving care I received from Jerry and Christine. Not once was I yelled at, scolded, or told I was stupid— although I was. Only in retrospect do I realize how damaged I was.

*

When I was a week out of the hospital, Elisabeth called. She'd already sent flowers but she wanted to know how I was managing. Did I need anything? What could she do? Was Jerry okay?

That's when she told me that she too had had strokes. We talked about the part nicotine played in plaque build-up in arteries. I told her

I'd quit. No cigarettes since I went to the hospital. She repeated her favorite retort: "Tend to your unfinished business and cigarettes can't hurt you."

I'd bought into that explanation because it came from Elisabeth, an esteemed medical doctor and psychiatrist. It had offered just the excuse I needed to continue my pack-a-day habit. Post-stroke, I no longer believed all illness resulted from unresolved emotional issues or trauma. It became evident that the body keeps score; abuse it and breakdowns happen.

In Elisabeth's letter of March 8, 1989, she spoke again about smoking. Due to additional strokes, she had received strict orders to stop both coffee and cigarettes, an affront: "My only two pleasures. I feel everything is being taken from me. Some weeks I'm down to eight cigarettes a day. Then, like today, I'm up to a pack."

*

The weeks before I returned to work, I'd wake up every morning with a to-do list in my head. While Christine and I ate breakfast, I'd tell her of errands I needed to run: grocery shop, go to the library, stop by the police station to say hello to the girls, maybe buy a summer outfit.

She'd say, "Sounds great Mom. Go get dressed. I'll drive."

When I undressed to get into the tub (no showers until the neck bandages came off), the sensation of air touching my nude body felt new and exciting. I had to dance a little to celebrate. Water was interesting, the way it formed around my body and swished. It dripped off my inverted fingertips like long fingernails. When the bath cooled, I experienced again air-nakedness, but this time wet nakedness, which called for a longer dance. When I was finally dressed, Christine and I headed for the car.

"Here's your purse, Mom," she'd say. On a cool day she'd guide me into a sweater. We'd get half way to town, seven miles away, and I'd start to cry.

Christine offered a solution, "How about we just get an ice cream cone and go home?"

"But I have so much to do," I'd say. "I promised the girls I'd stop by."

"They'll understand. I'll call them." Next, we'd drive through McDonalds. With ice cream cone in hand, I'd let my to-do-list melt away.

My cardiologist allowed me to return to work after six weeks. My physical state had never been better: no smoking, walking two miles a day, and I'd dropped a few pounds. Everyone, on first meeting, remarked how well I looked.

Although I thought I was back to full functioning, I was not. I couldn't grocery shop. My cart would be less than a quarter full when all the colors, shapes, and people over-stimulated me. I'd abandon my cart and leave the store, often in tears. Or, I'd get as far as the cashier; she'd greet me or ask a question and I'd cry and run out. Sometimes I couldn't leave because I couldn't find the door. To complicate this situation, I never expected shopping to be troublesome. Forgotten were all the other times I'd tried to shop and failed. I was an adult competent woman. With list in hand, I'd drive to the market, park the car, enter the store, and be shocked and confused when I couldn't complete my task.

At my dispatch desk I was unable to remember routines until I'd been back on the job six months. That's when I realized my co-workers had been covering for me. This made me angry. I yelled at my boss, "How will I know I've made a mistake if you don't tell me?" It hurt that they didn't trust me enough to give me honest feedback.

Despite evidence to the contrary, my self-image remained untarnished. Yes, I'd had a health bump, but I was still me: loving wife and mother, the counselor and facilitator of groups, a respected lecturer, a competent dispatcher, a smart woman. I knew stuff.

Jerry kept believing I was functioning just fine. On the other hand, when I spoke by phone to my daughter Janet, who was still living in NY, she gave me a different response. Before the strokes, we spoke weekly, but afterwards her calls came less often until they stopped altogether because our conversations often ended with me crying and her saying, "You're not the mother I've always known." She was in recovery from alcoholism and feeling fragile, yet I was saying anything that came into my head, including what she took as very mean judgments of her. "You have no filter!" she shouted. Her calls became so painful that for a year she communicated only through post cards with "Remember, I love you!" scratched on the backs. She and I stood on opposite sides of a chasm. She wanted me to be her pre-stroke Mom.

I thought I was.

*

Eventually the combined feedback from daughter Janet and the job forced me to consider that perhaps I was not seeing things clearly. Testing was in order, but what kind? I'd had CAT scans. Damage to speech centers was the only injury they caught. What other kinds of tests were there?

Occupational testing was suggested and I needed a referral to the only testing facility in Anchorage. Until then, it hadn't occurred to me that my surgeon should have ordered testing before clearing me to return to work. Under pressure from me, my GP made the referral.

On the day of testing, I was scared. Jerry and I entered a large, cold building and were met by a friendly young woman who would conduct my tests. The first battery was verbal. I felt I did well. I knew most of the answers. Maybe this was all unnecessary after all.

Next came reading comprehension and I was lost. I started to cry. Shape matching and placing colored pegs into coded holes reduced me to sobs. Jerry said, "That's enough."

The results came a week later. On the verbal, safety- related questions I scored at twelfth-grade level. That meant if I came home and found I was locked out, I knew enough to go to a neighbor's house and ask for help. When it came to reading comprehension and manual skills, I scored at or below sixth-grade level. Rather than deflated, I was relieved. Almost a year after the first whale sighting, I finally got a bearing.

Therapy seemed the next step; I called the testing facility to sign up. The therapist said, "You're not a viable candidate. It's been more than six months. The window for improvement is past."

"What am I to do? Is there no hope?"

"Challenge yourself daily," she said. That answer felt like no answer, like when my grandmother would answer a question with a nonsensical rhyme. "Keep on doing what you're doing," said the therapist.

That's all I heard, so I did it.

What I had been doing for years was to start my day with a book. I returned to that routine: sit with a cup of tea, open a book, find my place. Very familiar and satisfying. That I didn't understand what I read did nothing to diminish my pleasure. I was a reader, reading. I started on Homer's *Odyssey*. Why the *Odyssey*? Who knows? It seemed important. Much later I thought maybe this was a little joke from the Angels, because I was struggling with a personal odyssey to find or remake myself.

Individual words had meaning, but my short-term memory was such that sentences were lists of words, not linked messages. It was only after I'd regained some ability did I realize what I'd been missing. Once I started to understand an *Odyssey* paragraph, I realized I'd been reading that same paragraph for weeks.

I talked to my boss, who moved me into a clerical position. If it became necessary that I answer a call at dispatch, my colleagues monitored me. If the call involved life-threatening circumstances, it was transferred to another dispatcher. Due to the generous help of those wonderful women at the Palmer Police Dispatch Center, I was able to continue to work until I could retire with all my benefits.

Healing a damaged brain is a slow process. At my chiropractor's suggestion, I received weekly full-body massage for a year. After the first massage, I felt as though I came back into my body. With what I know now about brain function, I believe the massages stimulated brain cell production. I'm no scientist, so it may not be true, but it's a theory I choose to believe.

While the medical stuff was happening, I thought I was living life as usual. I worked, kept house, took pictures by the hundreds. Later I would understand that I was operating with what I see now as extreme naivete and frequently put myself into situations beyond my ability to handle.

One day in the late summer of '89, only four months from retirement, I went to the University of Alaska in Anchorage to use their photo lab. Although enlargers all work basically the same, and I was experienced with them, I couldn't make my prints. Disappointed and confused, I packed my things and tried to leave the building. I asked for directions but was unable to follow them. Once I made it outside, I wandered around and couldn't find my car. It was edging toward evening when I heard my name called. "Jan, what are you doing here?"

"Do I know you?" I was sure I'd never seen this small young woman in my life.

"I'm Brenda. We met at the LDT last January," she said. "What are you doing? Can I help?"

Brenda's description of me from that day is "confused and frail." She says I handed over my purse and book-bag without question and allowed her to take me to her home despite the fact that I didn't really know her. After I'd rested, she called Jerry and he drove into Anchorage to pick me up. I have no memory of how my car got home.

This was not an isolated event; it was repeated for years. I'd enter a public building fearless, a task to accomplish and no question about my ability to complete my mission. Each time I found myself lost and in tears, I was surprised. Perhaps the gift of poor short-term memory was that I didn't live in fear. Every day was full of possibility and promise.

*

After I retired, Jerry and I moved to Arizona to help my mother, who had been widowed four years before and was living in a half-finished house alone. We moved in with her, and five years drifted by as we finished the house and sorted and cleared the property. Physical labor gave me a great deal of satisfaction. We enjoyed nearby Prescott with its frontier atmosphere. It had a tiny airport and other services we might need, including a photo shop.

I was content, but my intuition had left with other abilities. No Angels whispered in my ear; the pen was dead. I couldn't gauge others' emotional states or reactions accurately. I seldom spoke in groups. Counseling was no longer a possible career choice. Three years post-stroke, sometime in 1992, I decided to take a customer service job in the one-hour retail photo lab. The equipment was mostly automatic and my experience in manual labs put me in good standing. I was employable!

During these years, whenever a letter or the Elisabeth Kübler-Ross Foundation Newsletter appeared in my mailbox, I'd be excited. That lasted only until I remembered I was no longer part of the organization. I longed to be back in the mix. I wondered what my co-facilitators thought of me, based on my behavior at my last LDT. Did they really miss me as they said? Shame, sadness, and longing would steal my pleasure, and I'd drop the letters into a file unanswered.

CHAPTER TWENTY-THREE

Becoming Leota (again)

MARIA, my boss at the photo shop, knew only that I was retired, bored with long days at home. She hired me because I knew photography. She flooded me with compliments about my skills, but I shrugged them off, unsure if she was being truthful. During my second month, Maria confronted me about my reluctance to accept her positive evaluation of my work. That's when I told her of my strokes and that taking the job was a test. I needed to know if I could learn. Could I retain sequential instructions and transform the steps into action?

Then I shared my prior work history and my training with Elisabeth.

Maria was one hundred and four pounds of passion: save the planet, feed strays, confront injustice, and above all care for one's friends. Elisabeth's name had barely left my lips when, in typical Maria fashion, arms waving, volume cranked up, she exploded, "I knew it! I knew you and Sondra had to meet."

Sondra was a photographer and a breast cancer survivor. I'd printed photos from rolls of film labeled with her name and wished with each frame that I had taken those photos. Her photographer's eye was unique and her exposures perfect. Secretly, I hated her.

"Perfect!" cried Maria. "She'll be in today to pick up her vacation rolls." For Maria the subject was closed and she was on to her next task. Chemical levels had to be checked, temperatures charted and prints sorted.

I ground my teeth. What did Maria expect of Sondra and me? Were we to compare and contrast our tragedies?

Bells clanged and I looked up to see a woman in the doorway supported by arm braces, the kind I associated with polio victims. Swathed in mauve wool, she was wrestling with the heavy shop door. "That's okay, I've got it," she called. It was a struggle but she managed. At the counter she smiled and said, "Hi, I'm Sondra. Are my rolls ready?"

Maria flew from her cubbyhole and made introductions. I nodded and busied myself locating Sondra's print order. I heard Maria tell Sondra that I'd been schooled by Elisabeth Kübler-Ross. Sondra paled. It was evident she knew of Elisabeth's work, and that meant Maria had identified Sondra as a cancer patient. Her back stiffened as if to withstand an onslaught of unwanted information. Her eyes dulled and silently seemed to plead, Please ... don't try to help me.

I felt empathy for Sondra immediately because Maria had unknowingly delivered the ultimate insult: she'd ripped from Sondra her unique identity and labeled her a disease. Both embarrassed, Sondra and I looked at each other. She recovered first, straightened her shoulders and said, "Interesting."

I said, "I've printed your rolls. You captured a mood with that long shot of autumn color under the stormy sky. I'm jealous."

After Sondra left, Maria started in. "What are we to do? I know Sondra is in denial."

"Denial about what?" I asked.

"Her cancer. That she's dying."

"So? What's the problem?" Maria was clearly upset and I didn't know why.

"I've read the books. I know the stages. Denial, Anger, Bargaining, Depression, and Acceptance.

Sondra is in Denial. She talks as if she's going to get better. Last week she was making plans!"

"So?" I asked.

"Doesn't she have to go through all the stages?" Maria's voice climbed an octave.

"Trust me, she will, in her own perfect time. She's been caretaking this disease for years. She knows what she's doing. She gets to be the authority. What's the advantage if you go in there and demand that she admit she's dying? How is that better?"

"But what are we to do? How are we to help?"

"Be her friend. Visit. Talk about what she wants to talk about. Do practical stuff she can no longer do, like lifting, or shopping when she's too weak. Listen and she'll tell you what will help. Maria, there's no wrong way to die."

I sensed that Maria wasn't convinced. Inside, I was giggling. A feeling of power surged through me. I knew what to say! I knew what Sondra needed. I knew what was best. It was as if I had located a compartment of my brain that was intact, pre-stroke intact.

Three years I'd wandered, lost in a world that made little sense, and suddenly I was standing on firm ground. I saw the situation clearly. My responses were natural and on the mark. In this tiny arena I was trustworthy.

*

On an autumn day, months after we'd met, Sondra and I sat in her Arizona kitchen. We talked pictures like fishermen talk fish—the ones we longed to catch, the ones we caught, the ones that got away. "I'm dying, you know" came at me unexpectedly, just before, "You want to see my favorite self-portrait?" She slid a four-by-six snapshot from under her placemat and handed it to me. The honesty of the shot stole any comment I might have tried to make. "I took that ten years ago. My first dance with Big C. That's when I thought I could win."

The months of silence had ended. The vertical photo had the orange cast of an old picture in which the colors had shifted. The background was open shelves. On the top shelf lay four books, flat, one on top of the other. Their titles: *Breast Cancer*; *Prevention*; *How I Conquered CANCER Naturally*; *BodyMind*. Sitting atop the books were three medicine or vitamin supplement bottles and one vial. Larger bottles filled the shelf to the right and continued out of the frame. On the lower shelf, bottles were stacked four high and filled the frame behind Sondra. Columns of bottles appeared to sit on her right shoulder and on her left shoulder. In the center, Sondra sat ram-rod straight, expressionless.

She looked directly into the lens, head shaven and naked. The frame ended just above her breasts.

We drank tea and talked about the photo, the composition, the story it told.

She asked about Elisabeth. "What do they do at her workshops? Do they help?"

"There's one coming up in the spring. It's in Scottsdale."

"Are they expensive?"

"I'm sure you'll be granted a scholarship if you ask."

We both knew that by spring she'd be too weak to manage the trip to Scottsdale on her own. Without telling Sondra, I'd decided to request a scholarship as well. If granted, I could be her companion.

*

Sondra managed the trip to Scottsdale better than either of us expected, though she missed much of the workshop itself due to her weakened state. She was in pain but excited and able to work on the mat. The on-site nurse and workshop staff checked on her frequently.

While Sondra was being facilitated in a private bedroom, I—unknowingly, and unexpectedly—embarked upon my own transformation.

My mat session consisted of revisiting my baby sister's death when I was two-years-old. What exactly happened next is unclear. I was on the mat one minute, and the next I was in an ambulance being transported to a Scottsdale hospital. On that ride, I acted frantic.

No one at the hospital noticed that I was in an altered state, that I was suddenly two-years-old confined to a hospital bed. With hospital staff I behaved like an angry toddler. I complained the thermometer hurt my mouth, tried to look behind the curtains that surrounded my bed, touched and fiddled with anything I could reach. The nurse tried to give me a shot, and I screamed, "No," hugging my arm to myself. Before long, I was considered in good health and released.

It took years for me to understand that the scene at the hospital was important. I'd stayed in my altered state from the mat session and acted out the frustration of a two-year-old—an extension of the mat process. I had to finish, to re-live forgotten experience.

Even in retrospect, the process still seems vague, yet as if it had great meaning. In the ambulance, I must have returned to the time I was standing beside my mother at the baby's grave, my two-year-old self reacting to Mother's grief. I knew, without truly understanding, that the baby was beneath that freshly turned soil, all alone in a plain box, or maybe not even in the box any more. Maybe she was in her fuzzy blanket with dirt in her nose and eyes and mouth. Terrified, I'd probably grabbed Mother's legs and thrown a full-blown two-year-old tantrum just as I did with the medical workers.

Today therapists employ similar methods in what is called experiential therapy wherein they regress the patient back to an earlier age and trauma. Even without clear guidelines, the LDT staff did everything right and kept me safe without reprimand. When we returned to the workshop site in Scottsdale, they directed me to bed.

The next day I woke in a cheerful mood.

On the drive home with Sondra, I shared my mat experience of being two-years-old. That's when the feeling struck me: it was time to reclaim my birth name, Leota. The idea felt radical—after all, I'd been Jan for nearly six decades—but it also felt exactly right. When I said "Leota" aloud, a calm solid feeling flowed through me. With no thought of how husband, mother, children or siblings would react, I became Leota.

Eventually I came to see how the name change connected to my mat session. My grandma, Dad's mother, was part Cherokee and Chickasaw and had given one of his sisters a traditional tribal name: Leota. Dad named me in honor of that favorite sister, who was childless. Mother didn't like Aunt Leota's nickname, which was Aunt Otie, and declared I'd be called Janet, which became Jan when I grew up. Even so, Grandma kept insisting on calling me Leota—until I was two. Then she caved in and called me Janet like everyone else.

After the mat session when I had regressed to age two so intensely, I thought about how that two-year-old child grew up into the adult Jan. Then, strokes changed me. I bore only a superficial resemblance to the person named Jan who used to be the Alaska Coordinator. My personality had undergone a major overhaul, and I was now a different person. In fact, that radical change resulted in the loss of my close relationships, except family.

In some kind of way, like my baby sister in the grave, the Jan I used to be was dead. By becoming Leota, I could stop trying to be the person I used to be and be who I was now: Leota.

CHAPTER TWENTY-FOUR

Sondra's Journey

IN DEFERENCE to Sondra's needs, we left the LDT early and returned home, where Sondra's final journey would soon begin.

Maria and I worried about Sondra being without family in Arizona. We were her only supporters. How would we manage when she entered the final spiral and was too weak to live independently? Her family lived in Michigan and wanted her home, but Sondra would have none of it.

Sondra had left Michigan after her doctors said, "Nothing more to be done." Against her family's wishes, she'd moved to Arizona to be near a popular guru/healer she had once spent time with, and who she believed was her romantic partner. For over a

Sondra

year she carried on a phone and letter campaign that today might be seen as stalking, all to no avail. She made excuses for his silence, insisting his staff withheld her messages because of jealousy. "If he'd received them, he'd surely call," she insisted. "Just a word, that's all I want." She was adamant she couldn't leave Arizona without his approval.

A few days after the workshop I found her weeping; still no return call or letter from Mr. Wonderful. She and I spoke openly about her diminishing strength, about her children who lived in Michigan along with her parents and lifelong friends, and about her life before Mr. Wonderful.

We negotiated. She agreed that five days was a reasonable time to expect him to answer her latest letter. If at the end of five days there was no word from him, she'd make plans to return home. His non-response would be her closure.

Five days sped by. Maria and I helped her pack. To conserve energy, Sondra would fly out of the Prescott airport rather than be driven two hours to the larger Phoenix airport hub. I had to watch the shop, so Maria took her to the small local airport.

After seeing Sondra's plane lift off, Maria returned to work. "You won't believe what just happened," she sputtered between hiccup-laughs.

"What?"

"We entered the tiny airport at Prescott

and guess who was standing right there? Mr. Wonderful, in all his ghostly-splendor!" She was referring to his pale complexion, white hair, and long white robes. Maria and I joked that it wouldn't be long until he'd be invisible.

We found out later that he and Sondra sat next to one another on the short connecting flight to Phoenix. A few days later, when I spoke with Sondra, she smiled into the phone and explained he'd been her teacher, not her lover. She'd misread his intentions, he said. All those times they'd had sexual relations at his seminars, he was merely helping her get over her sexual hang-ups, nothing more.

I wanted to throttle the man.

Sondra entered the Michigan hospital a few days later for a brief stay, then returned home and died shortly afterwards with her family beside her.

Occurrences like Sondra's were not unusual. It seemed magic hung in the air when an individual drew close to death. A patient would die minutes after a distant relative arrived at the deathbed, or during the five minutes the wife stepped out of the room. Long lost treasures, meaningful to the patient, would be found and returned just in time. Each experience is unique to that patient or that family.

Of course Elisabeth had an explanation, "There are no coincidences," she'd insist. "Guides, Angels, or even God, arranged it."

If she'd been at the airport with Sondra, she'd have said, "Sondra's guides arranged for her to complete her unfinished business." Maybe they did.

*

Months after the Scottsdale LDT, I began to contemplate my return to the field of counseling. At every turn I met a new acquaintance who'd benefit from Elisabeth's techniques. To practice in Arizona, though, I needed to return to college and earn a degree in order to qualify as a therapist. I wasn't sure I could learn from textbooks; hands-on, like in the photo lab, was very different from absorbing written information in a book. In the end, jealousy—what Elisabeth called the great motivator—made the decision for me.

A woman photographer, who frequented the photo lab, set my teeth on edge. Her photos were second rate. Mine were better. Yet she pasted hers onto card stock, placed them in every tourist trap in town, and they sold. Meanwhile, my shots sat home in a box.

That wasn't the worst of it; she bragged that as soon as she completed her degree, she would be counseling new mothers on child development. I was livid. From conversations I'd overheard between her and her daughter, her preferred parenting tools were intimidation, manipulation, and violence. I cringed to think how she might treat young mothers, let alone what she'd teach them.

My parenting style was to reinforce desirable behavior, distract the child from unwanted behavior, and never use violence. I wanted that counseling job. I had lots to offer. I would be great.

With this awareness came the need for action. I enrolled in one class at the community college, a test. I was terrified. Could I learn from a textbook? Would I be able to pass exams?

I completed the courses required and became a qualified therapist in Arizona.

*

At the five-year anniversary of my strokes, it was as if a switch was thrown. I woke with knowledge I didn't have the previous evening. Memory deficits lingered, but I could reason sequentially. The world became clearer. I understood things I had not just weeks before. I felt ready to step into a group as the facilitator.

My first post-stroke counseling position was the job the second-rate photographer thought she'd bagged: teaching at-risk mothers about childcare and development. My three children, now adults, lived in distant states and were childless, so these mothers became substitute offspring with whom I'd share lessons life had taught me.

According to Erikson's Stages of Psychosocial Development, the task for late adulthood is sharing wisdom. In the absence of my own children/grandchildren, these young women and infants allowed me to move naturally into my age-appropriate stage. No job, before or after, gave me such deep satisfaction.

*

As I moved forward, Elisabeth seemed to move backward in her career. In one letter she wrote, "I have no joy nor love nor laughter in my life for a long time. I don't think it is a result of the stroke. It is just that because I'm retired, I spend my life answering mail and am not able to be retired and keep my Center afloat and self-supporting."

I could hardly believe this statement came from the woman who'd spent her life teaching unconditional love as an attainable goal. It was impossible for me to imagine Elisabeth unloving or unloved and without laughter.

Additional strokes toppled Elisabeth. In 1995, while on a speaking tour in Paris, she suffered a severe stroke and cancelled the remainder of her speaking engagements. The tone of her newsletters changed and she started to report personal problems.

I heard from a staffer that Elisabeth's behavior had become unpredictable, and when concerned staff members attempted an intervention, it met with dire results: Elisabeth fired everyone. This brought to mind the personality shift I'd suffered after my strokes, though her situation was worse. She had suffered more strokes over a longer period of time.

A year later, Elisabeth's home in West Virginia burned to the ground with all its contents, and she suffered a paralyzing stroke. Rumors flew that certain neighbors in West Virginia—who objected to Elisabeth's plan to open an AIDS nursery—set the fire, though the final report from investigators stated that the wood-burning stove was the culprit, a verdict I believe Elisabeth resisted.

The Elisabeth Kübler-Ross Foundation closed, the farm was sold, and her son, Kenneth, moved her to Scottsdale, in Arizona, where he lived. Remembering Elisabeth's words "There are no coincidences," it was ironic that she spent her last ten years bed-ridden when her life's work was to raise awareness about the treatment of patients in this same vulnerable situation.

Although Elisabeth and I had not spoken in several years, she was never far from my thoughts. The principles I'd learned through the externalization process allowed me to navigate life's pains in a proactive way. Facilitating at LDTs had taught me to examine my emotional reactions. When the intensity didn't match the event, I'd know to look for a hidden cause of unfinished business. Usually I found a denied emotion: guilt, anger, grief, jealousy, or fear.

I had learned that it takes courage to dive into an emotional storm and experience the old putrefied feelings. To do so discharges stored emotional pain and leads to self-discovery and the ability to change negative beliefs. With self-knowledge comes authenticity, I think, and this frees an individual to take action. He/she/me is no longer compelled to stay stuck in react mode.

When my mother died, acquaintances thought that because of my training I'd be spared the pain that comes with a parent's death. The opposite was true. Knowledge allowed me to feel my loss and to know it was healthy. I knew what to expect and how to endure the crush of grief that comes wave after wave.

I couldn't have managed my life if I hadn't become a disciple of Elisabeth Kübler-Ross.

CHAPTER TWENTY-FIVE
Funeral

THE MORNING OF August 25, 2004, I had just
poured my second cup of tea when the phone rang.

Without preamble, my sister announced,
"Your friend Elisabeth died yesterday."

"Who died?"

"Elisabeth Kübler-Ross died. I thought since
you don't get a newspaper you may not know."

My stomach dropped like in a fast elevator.
"You're right. I didn't know." My hand started to
tremble. I set my cup down.

My ever-efficient sister rattled off the date,
time, and place for the funeral. I couldn't take it

in; my thoughts were elsewhere. Elisabeth died on my son's birthday. I flashed on the carved moose-horn ring he'd made for me when he was ten and how that ring was a factor in bringing Elisabeth and me together.

Travis turned thirty-five the day Elisabeth died. Was there a message here for him? He'd never met her, probably didn't know much about her work. Had she and I met thirty-five years ago? No, it'd been only twenty-five. Unable to make any further connections, I let it stand as a reminder of the mystical side of our relationship, Angels and all.

"You're going to the funeral, I suppose," Sis said.

I didn't know how to answer. Would I attend? So much had changed since I'd seen or talked with Elisabeth. I'd not worked for the Elisabeth Kübler-Ross Foundation since my strokes in 1988. In fact, the Foundation no longer existed. It had been years since I'd corresponded with any of the old staff. Would any of them be there? Last I heard, they'd all been fired in one big fiasco, because they were trying to take care of Elisabeth and protect her reputation. Would I be welcome at the funeral? There might be guards at the door to check IDs and turn away previous staff members who'd fallen into disfavor. My head was a hive of too many buzzing, stinging thoughts.

I counted off reasons not to attend: I was no longer the Alaska Coordinator; I lived in Arizona now. The Elisabeth Kübler-Ross Foundation, as I had known it, no longer existed. Lost were my close ties with other facilitators and individuals devoted to the principles and practices of her teachings. Those were the external differences, but what of the internal ones?

Although I still held to Elisabeth's teachings and applied them in my personal and professional life, no one from the present newly constituted Foundation would know me. Even my name was different. I was as different from the Alaska Coordinator as my two states, Alaska and Arizona.

When my head cleared, and I connected with my heart, the decision became easy. There was only one right choice. I had to make the effort and let the experience be what it was to be, regardless of outcome. To be true to Elisabeth's life-work, true to my core values, true to the process I based my life on, I would attend Elisabeth's funeral. If I was turned away at the door, so be it.

September 4, 2004, dawned cool and sunny in northern Arizona, a perfect day for the two and half hour drive down the mountain to Phoenix. Usually I found this drive pleasant. The sparse landscape ruled by majestic saguaro cacti led me back to my childhood and my Dad's enthusiasm for his new state—a time when the cacti grew free and unmolested by subdivisions and automobile exhaust.

However, on this day I was denied this pleasurable interlude because fear crowded into my Volkswagen bug. I wouldn't be able to find a parking place. No one would know me. Maybe they wouldn't let me in. It's for family only. I don't have an invitation. After all, my fear told me, Elisabeth was a global celebrity, who are you to expect to be welcomed? If they do have a list, your name won't be on it. What if there's a scene? Save yourself the trouble, turn around and go home.

I argued with my fear and tried to reassure myself. I was only making the effort; it didn't matter if I was turned away. My obligation was to show up. The outcome was out of my control. By the time I drove into the parking lot at the Scottsdale Bible Church, I felt calmer. I was surprised by the number of empty parking spaces. Was there a poor showing? Or was it evidence that attendance was limited? At first I felt lost; then I noticed a small hand-painted sign with an arrow, directing visitors to a chapel.

I was greeted at an outer entry and handed a program that listed names of the presenters and order of events. Odd how comforting it was to hold that folded creamy cardstock with familiar quotes and pictures. It affected me like an anxiety-reducing pharmaceutical, not to mention the relief that attendance wasn't restricted.

In the spacious entry, there were several lecterns, which meant no one had to wait in line to sign a guest book. As I stood with pen in hand, I was flooded with emotion. It surprised me that I didn't feel sadness or loss. Instead, I felt gratitude. My tears began to flow, the first since hearing of Elisabeth's death, or transition, as she called it. My process had begun. I thanked Elisabeth for the direction my life had taken due to her influence, and I penned my personal goodbye.

Close by, easels held posters that displayed recent pictures of Elisabeth, and some with her grandchildren, Sylvia and Emma. I hadn't seen Elisabeth for many years and was saddened by the changes in her physical appearance; it was evident her last years had been difficult.

At each of several entrances to the chapel were huge tubs filled with ice and bottled water. I felt well cared for and could almost hear Elisabeth's lyrical accented voice say, "Take care of physical needs first."

The sanctuary was large; to my untrained eye, it could easily seat hundreds. On the sanctuary floor, centered in front of the raised area, was an open, unvarnished pine coffin. A nearby flower spray held an abundance of sunflowers and daisies arranged informally, a perfect refection of the Elisabeth I knew. Amid the flowers on stage was a poster-sized picture of Elisabeth in her garden wearing a fuchsia-colored shirt. She was crouched between banks of white daisies. This photo was the one most often used on the dust covers of her books.

There was no order imposed on the people who entered the chapel, no ropes or arrows, no one stood guard, no ushers directed traffic. Each of us had to find our own way, a suggestion that this is your experience, you make the choices, do what you came to do—another of Elisabeth's strongly held beliefs: "Our lives are a result of choices we make."

I walked to the front and joined five or so people waiting their turn to step up for private last-minutes with Elisabeth. Just as I started to step forward, a young woman in black, with two small children, stepped in front of me. The youngest child grabbed the edge of the coffin and chinned herself to see inside. No reprimand from the mother, no hurried embarrassed words about being careful or polite. The mother remained calm and supportive of the two girls as they looked at and touched Elisabeth. The mother allowed them to set the pace; the girls decided when to leave. I knew right away they were being allowed to be their authentic selves. How could it be any different when Elisabeth Kübler-Ross was your grandmother, or when she was your mother?

I had expected Elisabeth to be wearing the familiar wrinkled pants and shirt, topped off by a sweatshirt with a slogan or picture on the front, her hair sticking out this way and that, but I was greeted by an Elisabeth with hair combed smooth, and wearing a red-print silk dress. It was a bit jarring. After all, she'd attended black-tie receptions and met crowned heads of state in her wrinkled cotton uniform.

Letting my eyes measure the differences between this Elisabeth and the Elisabeth I had last seen, I ached with loss: loss of time, loss of who I was, loss of health, both hers and mine, and, most of all, loss of that generous, always authentic, soul that was Elisabeth. I appreciated again the truths that she taught, one of which was the need for loved ones to see the deceased's body. Here she lay, true to herself and her teachings, for all to see. I was moved from loss and sorrow to gratitude and respect.

Tears made it difficult to find a place to sit. When I walked up the aisle, a woman touched my elbow. "Would you like to sit here?" she asked. "I've come alone and would like the company."

She added, "Judging from your tears, you must be experiencing a great loss." How could I explain that some of my tears came from gratitude?

On the wall above the stage a slide show was in progress: The Photographic Journal of Elisabeth's Life. The pictures depicted her personal as well as her professional life. I was struck by the generosity of her son and daughter to share their mother so completely with all in attendance. Every nuance shouted, "We know your relationship to our mother was important too. We understand your loss, although we will never know you." Their thoughtfulness for others at a time of their own personal crisis spoke of great generosity. I was reminded of how Jackie Kennedy shared her grief with a nation.

Through the photos, I reconnected with my experience of Elisabeth and to an earlier edition of myself. I moved through how applying her truths to my life had transformed me. How I had been stretched by what I learned at the bedside of dying patients and their families. At the LDT workshop in London, I had learned to what extremes human forgiveness was possible when compassion blossomed between Holocaust survivor Jews—who survived because they passed as Germans citizens—and SS Guards, all in the same room, each telling their stories of pain and shame. I remembered how I felt when she called me after my strokes to tell me she'd had a stroke too. I treasured the letter she wrote me in which she told of her struggle to stop smoking after her strokes. Sadly, she lost that battle. She died a smoker. Who was I to deserve such a friend?

From the back of the chapel came the joyful sound of voices singing "This Little Light of Mine," and down the side aisle marched a choir of eight larger-than-life black women dressed in white and gold robes. Before they gained the stage, the audience was on their feet clapping and singing. The choir led us in song after song, all Elisabeth's favorites, and the uproar continued for fifteen minutes or so. One could easily believe we were opening a Life Death and Transition Workshop with Elisabeth at the front of the room enjoying every minute.

Pat McMahon, a local Arizona celebrity, gave an official opening. I don't remember any of what he said, only that it was brief, and I was thankful. Barbara, Elisabeth's daughter, followed him and read a loving and entertaining piece titled, "A Daughter's Reflections."

More singing followed, and a gentleman gave an accounting of Elisabeth's work. The testimonies continued for over two hours. We laughed. We cried. We sang. We remembered.

It was perfect. By the end of the service I felt uplifted, refreshed, and grateful.

Before we filed out of the chapel, I was calm enough to look beyond the stage at Elisabeth's pictures. It surprised me to realize the room was being remodeled, that the walls were bare sheetrock except for two words. On the wall, left-stage, in tall six-foot maroon letters was painted "Extreme Makeover." Had a painter brushed them up there to test the color? Was it Elisabeth's guides or her Angels or even God who had added their comment?

I'd rather think it was Elisabeth having the last word—one more way for her to say, "There is no death."

AFTERWORD

When I walked into the emergency room and saw my mom lying in the hospital bed looking frail and exhausted—with her husband Jerry at her side looking lost—I began to sense that her end was near. I had been dealing with my husband's cancer with the support of hospice care so I knew I needed to introduce hospice services into Mom's life. Our choices were two: submit her to more invasive medical procedures or place her into Marley House, a hospice in-patient home. Mom and Jerry chose Marley House.

The first time Mom mentioned Elisabeth Kübler-Ross to me, I was twenty-two years old. I was living on Long Island as an active alcoholic. I would "drunk dial" Mom on occasion and she would tell me to go to Alcoholics Anonymous. One day, she said she wanted me to attend a workshop (she would pay for) given by a famous doctor who dealt with the terminally ill. It was about Life, Death and Transition, and she thought it would change my life. I thought she was crazy, as usual, but I agreed to go anyway. I met Elisabeth Kübler-Ross and her staff, and I participated in a workshop exactly like the ones described in this memoir. The experience did indeed change my life. I believe I got sober a few months afterwards due to the deep emotional work I did on the mat. The workshop also gave Mom and me a common language and helped us talk openly about her own death and dying.

The time came to transport her to Marley House from the hospital. Once there, she was taken care of in such a loving and caring way that I knew—and she knew—she was going to be okay. When I visited her, she spoke of how wonderful the staff was and how the whole organization made her feel safe. We had many conversations while she was there. She'd been writing her memoir about her years working with Kübler-Ross, and we spoke about how important it was to finish it before she died. She said she wanted ten percent of all sales of her book to go to the Marley House because without them and without hospice in general she wouldn't have felt so safe and cared for. I found it a wonderful irony that this woman lying in the bed, my mother, was friends with the amazing woman who helped usher the concept of hospice into the United States and was able to benefit from it herself.

Mom died peacefully within a month after we had this conversation. I will be forever grateful for Elisabeth and her work that took the stigma off of talking about death, because I was able to talk to Mom openly and honestly while she was dying. We cleared up past hurts and shared our appreciation of each other. When she transitioned, I was with her. It was quiet and fast, but I had said everything I needed to say, and I believe she had said all she needed to say to me too.

I wasn't finished with her but she was finished with this life. She left this memoir behind. It wasn't completely finished at the time of her death but she belonged to a group of professional writers in Prescott, Arizona, who stepped in to help make this publication a reality. Thank God for Angels!

Janet E. Bontrager
Prescott, AZ
2015

MORE TO BE SAID. . .

Among Leota's writing we found finished essays and stories that enrich our view of her life. In them are compelling insights into her years in Alaska and her Kentucky childhood.

The trick is to discern from our reading how much of the stories are directly from Leota's life and how much has been embellished by her literary artistry.

Welcome to more original writings by Leota.

ALASKA

Momma's Moose

ANNA REFILLED Ed's cup and turned back toward the sink. "Ran into Sierra yesterday in Anchorage. She said Paul's going after their moose this weekend."

"Paul's a fool," Ed managed around a mouth full of waffle. "Moose's still too high. They won't be in the valley 'til after the first snow."

"It better come soon—freezer's almost empty." Her voice soft, barely audible, Anna spoke more to herself than to Ed.

"If you think I'm drag'n a dead moose halfway down a mountainside, you're dumber 'n you look!" Ed snarled and jumped to his feet with such force his chair fell over backwards. He grabbed his coat, kicked the chair and bolted out the door. The chair spun across the kitchen and struck Anna in the shins. She almost dropped the coffee pot. Her face flushed and she fingered the diamond stud on her earlobe. Outside, the truck door slammed, the starter grunted then caught. Anna didn't move until she heard the truck bump through the deep pothole at the end of the driveway and accelerate onto Marten Rd.

Another day in paradise, she thought, and returned the coffee pot to its niche, righted the chair then sat on it to examine her shin. It was going to bruise but luckily no skin was broken. What set him off this time, she wondered and absent-mindedly pulled at her earlobe. All I said was "... freezer's almost empty." No reason to get angry, so early in the morning.

Anna peeled freezer wrap from a lump of moose burger and put it to thaw in a shallow bowl. She glanced out the window above the sink and, as always, the view pulled her away from the chaos of her marriage. Her eyes traveled beyond the swing set in the sloping front yard of mowed weeds. No houses were visible, no human signposts. Just Anna and the green mountains with snow-dusted tops and the muskeg bog across the rutted dirt road.

She admired the dense growth of fireweed that grew at the bog's edge. Fireweed—Anna's calendar, her solace. In spring it was the first green color. It whispered a promise of brighter days ahead. July into August it sent up stalks of magenta flowers to heights of five feet that invited her to celebrate—dance along the banks of Alaska's salmon streams—to fill her freezer with life sustaining red fillets. September's frost turned the plant vibrant red, and the ripened seeds spun a white, silky filament. Anna heard the white-topped weeds shout, "Moose season. Hunt. Winter's here." Worry knotted her stomach. Ed out of work; no moose in the freezer. How would they manage?

A brown blotch in the fireweed on the other side of the bog jolted Anna from her daydream. *What is it? Could it possibly be? Yes, it's a moose! Does it have a rack?* She ran for the binoculars on the bookshelf. She scanned the muskeg perimeter, located the moose, was sure—fairly sure—it was a bull. The rack wasn't big, but any size rack would do.

She bolted to the phone. *Who can I call? Where's Ed?* Phone in hand, Anna froze—she didn't know. He'd been unemployed for over a month but she didn't dare ask where he spent his days. Damn, wouldn't you know it, a moose practically in our front yard and no Ed. "Son-of-bitch!" she said aloud, "I'll shoot the damned thing myself." Her mind raced. It can't be that hard. *I'm a pretty good shot with iron sights, and Ed's 30.06 has a scope—piece of cake.*

Back to the bookcase, she reached between it and the wall, grabbed Ed's 30.06, and drew back the bolt. *Empty, damn! Where does Ed keep the shells? Shit, I should pay more attention. His dresser. I know I saw some in his sock drawer.* In the bedroom, Anna ran to the dresser, jerked open the top drawer and spilled the contents onto the floor. On hands and knees she shuffled through socks, belts and handkerchiefs. Nothing but .22 shells. Nothing big enough to fit the 30.06. For an instant she considered her Smith & Wesson revolver in the nightstand but knew it wouldn't do the job. 30.06 shells, where could they be? *The bookcase. Why not? He puts everything else there.*

In the living room she pulled the coffee table across floral printed carpet to the bookshelf. Standing on it, she fished a box of ammo from the top of the shelves—a yellow box with green letters: Hi-Power 30.06 cartridges. *Bingo*!

With the rifle across her lap, she took one shell from the box, pulled the bolt back and inserted the tip of the bullet into the barrel. It went in crooked; it jammed. Try as she might, Anna couldn't get the bullet into or out of the rifle. *Shit! A winter's meat waiting to be harvested, and I can't get the damned gun loaded*. In the space of two breaths, she dropped the rifle to the floor, stepped over it, sprinted to the desk and returned with a ball-point pen. She inserted the pen under the bullet, pried it up and out of the opening. Without hesitation she pulled a different bullet from the box, measured it for length against the first—they were all the same. *Damn. Do something*, her brain screamed. *The Bakers. Paul should be home.*

She ran to the phone and dialed. "How do you load a 30.06?" she blurted.

"What's wrong?" Paul asked.

"Nothing's wrong. There's a moose standing in the muskeg across the road, but I can't get the damned gun loaded."

"Where's Ed?"

"Don't know."

"Want me to come shoot it for you?"

"It'll be gone before you get here. I'll shoot it. All I need's to get this damned gun loaded. I tried, but the bullet got stuck in the barrel and I never got it out."

"You don't put the bullet into the barrel," Paul said. "Push your finger down on the bottom of the opening created when you pull the bolt back. It will give, then spring back. That's the magazine. You push the cartridge straight through the opening and into the magazine. It will feed automatically when the bolt closes. Try it. I'll wait."

Anna dropped the phone; it hit the desk with a bang. She crossed to the rifle and quickly pushed a shell through the opening into the magazine, then another. It was so easy. She held the rifle in one hand and retrieved the phone with the other, "Got it. Bye."

On her way past the sink, she stopped at the window and checked to see if the moose had moved. *Nope, still there. But only the rump is visible.* His head was down. Alder bushes hid his front quarter. *OK, I'm really going to do this. What next?* She scoured her memory for any helpful tidbit left there by Ed's boasting of each year's kill. *I can't shoot across a road—that's illegal. OK, I have to cross the yard, go past the road, and get to the fence line without spooking him. If he sees me, he'll walk into the bushes and out of my freezer.*

Anna stepped onto the porch and pulled the kitchen door closed behind her. It closed with a loud click; she jumped. Was it always that loud? She stepped off the side of the porch by the wall and walked on tiptoes to the corner. Leaning against the sticky tarpaper siding she gripped the rifle hard, with both hands. She held it diagonally across her chest. Blood pounded in her ears. Her palms throbbed with each heartbeat. Her nostrils flared to suck in more air—air bloated with smells. Her chest came more alive with each gulp and her body felt lighter. She crossed the small open patch of lawn in a half crouch, keeping her head lower than the alders. Everything appeared edged in light; walking was easy, more like dancing than walking. And the smells: detergent, green-apple shampoo, onions and exhaust fumes mingled with grass and damp. Anna shivered and realized she had never felt so alive, so powerful. Now I understand. The hunter is invincible.

She reached the road and crossed it quickly, still bent from the waist like a soldier going into battle. She jumped from the road into the deep sponge of muskeg and was again assaulted by smells—crowberries, wet wood, decay. The muskeg sucked at her feet as she crossed to the fence. I'll wear boots next time.

She brought the rifle to her left shoulder, braced the barrel against the fencepost, and eased her eye to the scope. She checked for antlers but saw ears. The moose was looking straight at her, the ears swiveled. Did she see antlers? Yes... No... The scope turned green. Tilting the rifle down she found the head again. Yes, antlers, not much bigger than ears. Hurry! Hurry! Pull the trigger or he'll walk into the brush. But where to shoot? She lined the cross-hairs up just behind the shoulder, midway between back and belly. Was that right? Yes, shoot. Hurry, or winter's meat will walk away. She held her breath, cross-hairs steady, and squeezed the trigger gently. She didn't feel the blow to her shoulder that would leave a purple bruise, nor did she hear the shot. No kick, no sound, just the smell of burned gun powder. The scope went green.

Oh, my God. No… No! What have I done? I'm sorry. I didn't mean it. Remorse fell over her like a body bag. No apology would bring the bullet back. Once fired, a bullet had no conscience. Tears filled her eyes. Anna let the butt of the rifle fall to the ground. Holding onto the barrel, she leaned forward and vomited. The next black wave to overtake her was fear. She heard a car and dropped to the ground on her belly, numb to the wet that seeped through her clothes. The car sped by and out of sight. She picked herself up, and with rifle in hand she sprinted across the road, retraced her path, and skirted the lawn, keeping low behind the alders.

Back in the kitchen she threw the rifle onto the counter. It knocked the bowl of moose burger into the sink. The bowl broke and the meat lay among the shards. Her face was a mask of terror smeared with tears. Her clothes wet. Dead weeds clung to her front. Purple crowberry-blood spotted her chest—mock bullet wounds. She raced around the house, closed drapes, pulled shades, locked doors.

In one lucid moment she wondered, what am I afraid of? I didn't do anything wrong. I didn't kill anyone. The moment passed and her fear accused, "Murderer." *No... No. I didn't do it. It was only a moose. You don't have a hunting license. They're going to come get you, throw you in jail. It was a cow.*

Anna rushed to the bathroom and vomited into the toilet. Shaking and crying, she rinsed her mouth at the sink avoiding the mirror.

Gravel crunched in the driveway; the sound sent her into the closet. She squatted behind the coats and stuffed her shirttail into her mouth to stifle sobs. She heard heavy footsteps on the porch. Someone tried the door.

"Hey, open up," Ed shouted and beat on the door. Anna didn't move. Finally he stopped pounding and used his key. "Anna... you here? Why's the house shut up?" He saw the rifle on the counter, broken glass and moose burger in the sink. "Anna, where are you? Stop fooling around... This ain't funny."

With her toe, Anna pushed the closet door open but made no move to get up. Ed crossed to the closet and looked in at her huddled against the back wall. "Baby, what's going on? Did someone hurt you? Why is my rifle in the kitchen?" He reached down. She took his hand and he pulled her up and out of the closet. She collapsed against his chest. His scratchy wool shirt smelled of beer, cigarette smoke, and perfume. She didn't care.

"Come on. Stop crying. Tell me what's going on. What happened here today?"

"I shot a moose," she mumbled.

Hands on her shoulders, he stepped back and bent down to look into her face. "You shot a moose? That's great. Where is it?"

Anna stared at a stain on his shirt. "It's across the muskeg."

"How do you know you killed it?"

"The scope went green."

"It probably walked off."

"No, I think I killed it."

"The house all closed up, you hiding in the closet looking like you've been run over, all because you shot a moose?"

"I thought they were coming to get me, put me in jail. It was awful. Like I'd shot someone—a person."

"A person? You? Shoot a person?" He straightened, released his grip on her shoulders and crossed to the kitchen window. "That's a hoot—you couldn't shoot anyone."

But Anna knew different. She stood alone, head down, lost in memory. Her right hand pinched her earlobe and the diamond stud earring, hard and sharp, bit into her index finger. The earrings were a make-up gift Ed had given her after he'd used her ears as handles to slam her head into the floor as he sat astride her chest screaming, "I love you. I love you." Never again she'd promised herself. He'll never hurt me again. I'll point the pistol at him and he'll stop.

Anna had believed the Smith & Wesson would keep her safe. But as she stood frozen she watched a different scene play out as if it were a movie. Ed crazy mad-drunk came at her. She saw him pull his arm back, cocked, ready to fire his fist. Her hand went to the nightstand's top drawer and came up with the pistol. She held it in both hands aimed at him and yelled, "Stop." But he kept coming, eyes bloodshot, mouth drawn down into a sneer that hurled curses, "Bitch. Whore."

"Stop." she screamed again. He was supposed to stop. But he kept coming. Her finger tightened on the trigger. The gun fired.

Ed turned from the window distracted by a sound, a whimper. He saw Anna shudder. "What's the matter, Baby? You cold?"

"Yeah… cold."

"You better get out of those clothes, they're wet. Why are you wet?"

"Huh? Wet…oh, I fell …yeah… better change."

Halfway up the stairs Anna heard Ed switch on the evening news. In a solemn voice the channel-five anchorman said, "Today a mother of three was sentenced to life in prison for the shooting death of her children's father." Anna's knees buckled. She grabbed the banister for support. *That could've been me.* In the bedroom she crossed to the night stand, opened the top drawer and drew out the suede-leather gun case. She sat on the bed and unzipped the butterfly case to expose the Smith & Wesson .38 Special. It lay there innocuous but ready. A deep sob shook her body. The instrument she'd once seen as her protector had become a threat to Ed's life, her freedom and the children's well being.

She cradled the gun in her left hand and pushed the cylinder release with her right thumb. The cylinder swung open to expose six brass buttons. With her left index finger she drew the ejector rod back and the unfired cartridges fell into her lap. She collected the cartridges and fumbled in the top drawer for their box. Where can I hide these, she wondered. She remembered the old ribbon box on the top shelf of the closet, a keepsake from her favorite aunt.

With the cartridges hidden safely away, Anna returned to sit on the bed and used her shirttail to wipe her oily fingerprints off the gun before she zipped it back inside the case. She returned it to the top drawer. Without pause she brought the phone onto her lap and dialed her mother's number, "Mom?"

"Anna? Is that you? Have you been crying? Are you hurt?"

Anna cleared her throat, "No, Mom. I'm okay. Can me and the kids come stay for awhile?"

"Yes. Of course. But why? What's happened?"

"I'll explain when we get there. I need sorting and I can't do it here." Anna heard the door slam and the sound of running feet downstairs. "The kids are home from school, Mom. I gotta go. We'll be there tomorrow."

Anna pulled on dry jeans and replaced the crowberry stained shirt with her wildflower sweatshirt. The fireweed pattern was a faded pink and the cuffs stretched and threadbare— her butchering shirt. She dried her face and turned to check herself in the bathroom mirror. For just a moment, she didn't' recognize the image reflected there. Who was that tall, square-shouldered, capable looking woman? Where had the frightened, foolish girl gone?

From downstairs Anna heard the refrigerator door open and Ed called out, "Bring your ole Dad a beer."

Another evening in paradise, she thought, and started downstairs. Before she stepped into view, she took a deep breath, extended to her full height and adjusted her sweatshirt on her hips. At the landing she paused to shout, "Hey... Who's help'n Momma dress-out her moose?"

The Hunter

IT'S AUGUST and anglers from around the world converge on the Anchor River near Homer, Alaska. They come to fish for King salmon in the salt water and silvers in the river. For me it's simply time to stock the freezer. Determined to catch the day's first tide I roll out of my warm bed in the dim light of pre-dawn and pull on my long-johns, wool socks, jeans, sweatshirt, down jacket, and knit cap. I want to get there before Ralph or he'll be in my spot then he'll crow about it till end of season, "College professor beats local..." With him everything's a contest.

Around my hips I strap on my bait-box filled to the brim with irregular clusters of sugar-cured salmon roe from Tuesday's catch. My fingers on the buckle never fail to bring back the memory of five-year-old Jeremy's screech "Cookies!" as his chubby little hand snatched up a cluster of eggs and popped them into his mouth. He had the glob chewed and swallowed before I could stop him, and how he cried when I refused him a second one. I had to admit they looked good enough to eat, like lumps of cherry jelly laid out on newspaper. Wonder if Jeremy's finding any cookies these days. When his sister called last week she said she'd seen him panhandling on a street corner in downtown Portland. We have no more control over our spawn than does the salmon.

On the porch I pull on the essential—but hated—hip-waders; they must weigh five pounds each. I lift my rod off the nails where it hangs, strung and ready, under the eaves of the porch, and head for Slide Hole. My raised forearm shields my face as I plow through chest-high vegetation, and I remind myself to listen for sounds other than the slap and rub of wet brush against me. Other hunters use this river for winter's food too. I'd been reminded of that yesterday when I came upon a bear's paw print at the river's edge. And not three inches to the left of it was the print of a tennis shoe; two hunters looking for a meal.

The short walk has warmed me, but my exposed skin—cheeks, nose and the back of my neck—feels as if I've been sprayed with a cold mist. At the river's edge I can barely make out shadow forms of fishermen already in the river. We nod but no one speaks. The only sound is that of water moving over smooth rocks. I step into the river cautiously. The water isn't deep, but the current is swift. With the first step I feel the river's chill begin to penetrate my wool socks, and I know my feet will be numb before the fish arrive. I take care to set each boot before putting my weight onto it. So easy for a rock to roll, my foot to slip and I'd end up in the river—cold, wet, embarrassed, and with some angry neighbors. My spot's empty and I'm relieved. Now we wait.

My fellow fishermen, the trees, the water, and my hands, merge with the morning light. Using a knot I learned from my grandfather, I tie-on a clump of eggs. We stand statue like, all eyes on the river's smooth surface. The tide has come into the river's mouth, raised the water level and disguised the current. The water looks smooth and still. I hear the flap of a beaver's tail on the opposite bank.

Then I see it, a mini-tsunami-like wave about three inches high moving upstream, created by the massive fish coming in. From down river I hear, "Fish-on," and ready myself. I cast and feel my bait bounce on the bottom, then my line starts to move up stream. "Fish-on!" I cry. My companions on either side reel in their lines so as not to become tangled. My pole bends in a deep arch. I walk backwards towards the bank, I keep my eyes on the line where it disappears into the water. Five minutes, ten perhaps, and I gain the bank and a shiny silver slithers onto the mud at my feet. I slip my knife from its sheath and slice through each gill and wait while the fish bleeds into the hard-packed mud of the bank. I wiggle my toes to restore feeling and turn to watch my companions perform the "Fish-on" dance, each one in turn as if choreographed.

It's been a good run. Everyone caught their limit. After a few polite words are exchanged and promises of, "see ya later," we pick up our fish and leave the river, leave the other salmon to continue their heroic journey upstream to their spawning bed. We humans have filled our meager need. Now the eagles and bears will feast, and after them will come other scavengers—all hunters surviving off the bounty of salmon. Even the earth comes to the feast. After all the others are through, the soil will soak up nutrients from rotting carcasses to feed next year's vegetation, which in turn will feed small birds, rodents, and insects.

I cup my fingers inside the gills of my morning's catch. The tail drags on the ground as I slog my way back to the cabin. It's full light now; I'm cold and hungry. My shoulders ache. I miss Jeremy. Carrying our catch was his job after he grew into the task. Where's the justice? You feed, protect, and nurture your kids with the expectation they will want what you want—a family, a house, two cars in the garage and a boat. What went wrong? The counselor says to stop sending money. "Tough love," she said, "that's what's needed now."

Back at the cabin I set the coffee on to perk and trudge back outside to clean and fillet my fish. My timing is perfect; I get the last package wrapped and in the freezer just as the coffee boils. On a cold morning, nothing beats the smell of fresh perked coffee mingled with that of fresh-caught fish frying. The grill is hot, and without thinking I pour four puddles of pancake batter. What the heck, two for me and two for Mr. McNutt, the squirrel that lives in the fallen tree out front.

The stove turned off, the table set, and I ease my body onto the straight-backed, wooden chair with the cracked seat. All the furniture in the cabin is cast-off, not suitable for an everyday house but perfect for fish camp. The last of my energy spent, I sit still and let the coffee mug warm my fingers. I wonder what Jeremy's having for breakfast. Where does he sleep? Hunger overrides my fatigue and demands I eat. I butter and syrup the pancakes and fork off a bite of salmon. I dip it sparingly in syrup before taking it into my mouth. I'm grateful no one is here to witness my tears—tears of regret and gratitude. Tears of regret for how I must have failed Jeremy intermingle with my tears of gratitude for the surrender of this magnificent fish, gratitude to be alive in this pristine environment, gratitude for the ability to survive in this harsh land. I feel as if a deep, organic hunger is sated.

February Eighth

"FIRST SLIP the knife-tip in, just so. I promise the blood will flow you through the darkness into never-ending light," says the motherly clerk as she presses the knife's slim blade against the vein in Sara's wrist. Motherly clerk, a showroom of Never-Ending Lights, Ltd., and Sara, float through space inside a radiant sphere. Before Sara can ask if this is a sample of the promised never-ending light, the boys' muffled whispers and giggles reach into the dream and snare her. She is dragged from the warmth and bright lights of her dream into the darkness of Alaska in February, into an isolated homesteader's cabin seventy miles north of Fairbanks, and twenty miles north of the road's end. Her sons, Levi and Justin, have called her back.

Sara resists opening her eyes, savoring the sacred quality of her undisturbed morning bed. As long as her eyes are closed, she feels safe, in control. Braced, she opens her eyes, and she is lost again. Her internal darkness merges with the outer darkness, and she loses all sense of separateness. Darkness surrounds and fills everything, especially herself. Darkness owns the world. Sometimes Sara panics, because she can't tell if her eyes are open or shut. The degree of darkness is unchanged. Each morning she asks herself what is the difference between my darkness and the world's darkness. They seem the same. Only when she is armed with a lighted lamp, can she claim a tiny sphere of space for herself and the boys. But her claim is temporary. Blow out the lamp, and darkness owns all.

The dark controls time as well as space, erases the difference between morning, late afternoon, evening and night, A.M. and P.M. The impotent wind-up clock counts the hours by twelves, but is powerless to divide day from night. Sara and the dim light claim only four hours in the middle of the day, the hours between eleven A.M. and three P.M. Darkness owns the other twenty. Sara views these four precious hours as an elusive gift. Regardless of effort or sacrifice, she cannot bring the light earlier or persuade it to stay longer. The light makes but one requirement of her: to receive the gift, she must be awake. Because she must be awake to receive the light, she has come to view sleep as an enemy, an ally to darkness.

Sara shakes her head as if to clear her mind. She tells herself that it is morning now. Time to get up. She opens her eyes, and disappears into the darkness.

Once her eyes are open, Sara finds no benefit to lingering under the covers. Her oversized jeans and wool shirt are within easy reach atop her bed; they make a handy extra layer, and she can locate them without a light. To retain body heat, Sara pulls her outer clothes on over her long johns and wool socks while she's still under the covers.

Dressed, she stands, turns in the dark, and closes her bed covers as if to do so will conserve the heat until she needs it again. She knows well the four steps from bed to table. With no wasted movement she locates the matches and lights the lamp. Instantly the details of her daily life spring into being. The boys are in their bed along the opposite wall. Trying to quiet their voices, they have covered their heads with Grandma's heavy quilt made from worn out blue-jeans. The faded blue of the quilt matches the blue and white linoleum underfoot and the blue and white checked table cover.

The heating stove—a fifty-five gallon oil drum turned on its side with a cast-iron plate welded onto its top—waits in the corner for the wood she will add. Without thinking, she feeds the stove from the small pile of wood stacked in the shadow between the stove and the corner. Sara adjusts the damper and hears the flames catch as soon as she closes the door. She turns and crosses to the opposite corner into the kitchen area.

Facing the wall, Sara moves the pump handle up and down to bring water up from the well beneath the cabin. To the left of the pump-counter, which is covered in the same linoleum as the floor, are the homey faces of three women and a man pictured on a Norman Rockwell calendar. The calendar is the brightest spot in the cabin. The picture is alive with yellow sunlight pouring through the window of a small town butcher shop where the butcher and three women are visiting. More important than the picture, are the colorful X's drawn through the first seven days of February. As she fills the blue speckled enamel teakettle, Sara glances up from the sunny window of the calendar into her own window: curtainless, and so black it doubles for a mirror.

Beyond the mirror surface, Sara looks into the face of darkness and shudders. She drops her eyes back to the faces on the calendar.

Setting the teakettle atop the stove, she thinks of the millions of mothers the world over who are starting this eighth day of February with her, most of them in a world of sunshine and friends. She address two by name, "Hello, Mary Jo of Dakota, are you having any snow?" "Ciao, Christina of New York, what's the latest news?" Sara no longer feels silly conversing with her imagined friends; it keeps her sane, keeps her from feeling so alone. She knows she'll make it. She'll get herself and the boys through to spring. She'll keep things together until Wayne gets home from Fairbanks. She will not lose her mind. She will not use her mother's remedy. "Good morning you all, welcome to this the eighth day of February."

Justin's back-side hits the floor with a thump. He jumps up and attacks the lump under the quilt with flying fists, screaming, "Mommy, Levi pushed me. I didn't do nothing."

Levi's head emerges from under the quilt, his straight blonde hair alive with electricity, matching the energy of his words, "He kicked me first."

"Did not."

"Did too."

"Cut it out boys. Get dressed," says Sara. She applies the tip of the slender knife to the lid of an unopened box of oatmeal.

"Mom. Not oatmeal again," Levi whines.

"What's wrong with oatmeal? You like oatmeal. It's your favorite. Besides, no pancakes until Daddy brings more flour."

"Not for dinner. Not oatmeal for dinner. Can't we have moose stew? There's plenty left over."

"You know that's for dinner. We don't eat stew for breakfast."

"Mom, are you crazy or something? This is dinner!" Levi almost screams.

Sara glances at the clock, on a small shelf over the head of her bed. Six o'clock. Her stomach knots, and bile rises in her throat. "What? What do you mean, this is dinner?"

"Mommy," Justin whimpers, "You're scaring me."

Sara squats to Justin's height and strokes his back as she croons, "Okay, okay, Mommy's sorry. Nothing to be afraid of. It's just us chickens." All the while she's panicked, short of breath. Getting dizzy. Her mind is racing. It's 6:00 AM. It is. It can't be 6:00 PM. Was she finally losing it? Had she lost a whole day? Can't be. She remembers going to bed last night as usual. Or was it this afternoon? No, it was last night. It was. She clearly remembered Justin crossing yesterday off just before going to bed. Or did we all take a nap? Did she forget the morning? Did she lose a day's light, exchanged one day's light for another? What day is it? She had to know. Although her exterior is calm, inside Sara screams, "Help, Mary Jo! Help, Christina! Tell me, what day is it? Tell me I'm not alone. It can't be just me and the kids living this day, maybe a make-believe day—half one day and half another. It can't be. Tell me we are not alone."

Sara takes deep, slow breaths. "Stop it," she tells herself, "There are millions of women all over the world getting up to start this same day—February eighth. We're all doing the same thing, starting our day. There is Christina in an apartment in New York City, and Mary Jo on a farm in Dakota, and we are here, on the homestead in Alaska. We are all getting up on the same day. We are caring for our children. We are connected. It not just me and the boys out here all alone in the dark. Millions of people are getting up with us and sharing our day, the same day—February eighth. I'm not the only one."

"It's dinner time," Levi insists with the authority of a nine-year-old, "and we want stew. What's the matter with you Mommy?"

"Yes, what's the matter?" echoes five-year-old Justin. "We want stew."

"OK, OK. You can have stew." Sara puts the oatmeal back into its box. All the while she is thinking, what difference does it make if we eat stew for breakfast? Food's food, no matter what time it's eaten. Could it really be dinner? Could she have lost a whole day? She's in charge and she doesn't even know what day it is. Could Mary Jo and Christina have gone on without her? Are they starting today, tomorrow or yesterday? Or are they finishing yesterday or today? Was she trying to start tomorrow before they finished today? Has she been careless and slipped out of sync with the rest of the world? She would not let it be. Would not be the only one living this day-that-is-not-a-day. She would not.

As Sara pours the pan of boiling water, intended for the oatmeal, back into the teakettle, she says to Levi, "Get the stew from the ice-box if you want. But put on your coat first."

"Right." Levi's opens the cabin door. Light springs out through the open door onto the rough, unfinished boards of the cabin porch. The light cannot reach inside the crude wooden box that hangs on the outside cabin wall adjacent to the door. The box is insulated to protect the contents from freezing, except for the backside which captures escaping cabin heat. Levi reaches in among the shadows, locates the familiar stew-pot and returns to the kitchen—all without his coat.

Sara automatically sets the stew onto the stove's sweet-spot. So was it AM or PM? The clock was useless. The calendar wouldn't help either. The boys will want to X through February eighth just as if it were any normal day. They won't care if it's the right day or not. All they want is to mark off another day between now and April thirtieth when Wayne is due back. But she cared. She refused to live the wrong day.

Sara feels a sick-headache coming on as she takes the white pottery dishes from the shelves above the kitchen counter. Normally she would pause a second and admire how the white dishes looked among the yellow sunflowers of the shelf's paper, but today—what-ever-day—she has more important matters on her mind. Absent minded, she hands Levi the plates. On his way to the table he stumbles. One plate hits the floor with a bang, but doesn't break.

"Cut it out!" she snaps, then apologizes immediately. She tells herself, "Steady girl, don't yell at the kids. It's not their fault. You're the adult. You should know what day it is. You're the responsible one. It is up to you to keep things running. They're only little boys. They didn't ask to be brought out to this desolate place and holed up all winter, in the dark, with a crazy woman. Come to think of it, neither did you."

Garlic wafts from the luke-warm stew, calling the boys to the table. They slide into their seats sidewise, struggling, because they have pushed the chairs too close to the table. Just as the boys gain their seats, Sara remembers her ace in the hole. The radio. Her invisible link to the world. And since it is invisible, it can't be stolen by the darkness. She asks the boys, "How would you like to listen to the radio?"

"Oh boy, the radio!" exclaims Justin.

From Levi, "It's not Friday, Mom. Why the radio? Is something wrong?"

"No, this time we are not listening for a message. This time it is just for fun. It's because you boys have been on such good behavior."

"Right," answers Levi. He fills his mouth with stew.

Sara's voice is cheerful as she tell the boys, "You guys eat. I'm going out to start the generator." If she could get the darn thing started. But it was getting easier. She used to be exhausted after three or four pulls. Now she could keep it up for eight or nine tries. With the lifting, dragging and pushing, her arms and shoulders had gotten a lot stronger.

Sara slips into her reddish-orange down parka, the one she found pictured on page thirty-two of last year's Eddy Bauer catalogue; she zips it up to the neck then snaps the front closed. She sits on the ugly wooden bench just inside the cabin door and pulls on the four-pound snow-packs that Wayne called shoes. Shoes her ass—they were ugly, felt-lined rubber boxes and heavy as lead. And Wayne had mounted the shelf over the coat pegs so high she had to stretch to get the wool stocking cap, the leather gloves, and down-filled outer-mittens. Totally packaged, she opens the door and stares into the depth of darkness and remembers the flashlight. But before she can turn from the open doorway, darkness grabs her and holds her motionless. It is her personal darkness made external, the darkness of the grave. She is powerless. Cannot move.

"Close the door!" The boys' voices break the hold.

Bending her knees and dipping down, Sara grabs the square nine-volt light from under the end of the little bench, all the while staring ahead into blankness. She shifts the light into her left hand, steps out onto the porch, and closes the door behind her. She stands motionless, willing herself to breathe. The pain of minus thirty-degree air passing through her nose and into her chest helps her separate from the impersonal darkness. There are no night creatures to break the silence of this vast waste land of tundra, with its scrawny, deformed black spruce trees leaning against one another in an unsuccessful attempt to stand upright. Sara fumbles through her bulky mittens to switch on the light as she steps off the porch.

Shivers run up her back and her skin crawls from the squeaky sounds of her snow-packs in dry snow. She keeps her eyes focused on the snow within the scope of her light's beam. She has no desire to look up into the star engorged sky. She needs no pricks of light from millions of miles away to remind her of her isolation. She needs her pain, the squeaking snow, her quivering skin, and the flashlight to separate her from the darkness as she crosses the twenty feet from the cabin to the unpainted shed that holds the generator.

The shed door screams in protest as Sara pulls it open and steps inside. She looks at the generator on the shed's earthen floor. She had to get the thing started. She couldn't let the boys float in space all by themselves not knowing if it were day or night. She hangs the light on the wire hook attached to the ceiling, removes her outer mittens, checks the fuel level in the generator, and adjusts the throttle and choke to full on. She braces her left foot against the red foot of the generator, her right slightly behind for support, and bends to take the wooden handle of the starter rope in both her gloved hands. She breathes deeply and prepares herself for the effort of a forceful pull. She pulls toward her right hip with a quick, hard motion. The silence of failure is broken by the whirl-thud of the starter rope retracting. She braces herself for another pull. Silence, whirl-thud. A third pull and still nothing. On the fourth pull the generator pops. Sara adjusts the choke to half open and pulls again. The generator coughs, but does not start. The next pull is critical; if it isn't just right the generator will flood, and she will not get it started. She braces herself, takes a deep breath, concentrates with the single mindedness of an Olympic athlete, and pulls. The generator sputters, then catches.

The little shed fills with fumes and blessed mechanical throbbing. She hurriedly adjusts the throttle, waits a minute or two, then slowly closes the choke. Quickly, she draws on her outer mittens, grabs her light and runs for the cabin, leaving the shed door ajar.

Leaping onto the porch, Sara bursts through the cabin door. She enters into the glare of electric light coming from a single, bare bulb hanging from the cabin's ceiling. She throws her mittens off, not caring where they land, and crosses to the pink plastic radio on the shelf above the bed. Fully dressed for outside, her heart pounding in her ears, she stares single mindedly at the tiny radio. She doesn't try to name the song, a favorite game of hers, but waits impatiently for the music to stop and the announcer to speak.

Finally, an overly cheerful announcers says,

"There you have it folks, Hoyt Axton with his newest release "The Life Machine," and now for the weather report sponsored by Alaska's own Husky Batteries. To-day, the eighth of February, the high reached thirty below, and we gained two-and-a-half minutes of daylight. The forecast for tomorrow is clear and cold with four hours and seventeen minutes of possible sunshine. Stay tuned because coming up next is this evening's addition of the Mukluk-a-gram with messages to our listeners out in the bush. Remember, if you want to send a message, write it on a three-by-five card and mail it to Mukluk-a-gram in care of this station, at P.O. Box 80, Fairbanks."

Sara stares at the radio and repeats to herself, "It is evening. It is dinner time. It is 7:00 PM not AM." She begins to tremble, cold from the inside out. Was this how it began with Mother? Promises of never-ending light. Drifting off into space not to know one day from the other, morning from evening. Is this the beginning of an insanity that would end in death? Has darkness finally won?

KENTUCKY CHILDHOOD

Appalachian Christmas

CHRISTMAS 1943, I was five, my sister three, and brother one year old. This year was a special treat because Daddy said, "We're going to the farm for Christmas!" My paternal grandparents' home in Mt. Vernon, Kentucky—always referred to as the farm—was for summer visits only.

A winter visit? After it had been snowing all week? Never! Even in summer you couldn't get down the mile-long lane to the house by car. Folks in Kentucky didn't worry much about the lane as only my Daddy and one uncle had cars. We were the Ohio bunch. My Kentucky family and their neighbors walked everywhere, or used a wagon and mules to transport big loads.

The farm was my most favorite place to be. I felt important when Papaw put me up onto the back of Jenny, the gentle mule, who along with Bow pulled the wagon at haying time. The farm was where I helped Grams do the wash; first we boiled the white clothes in an oval cast iron cauldron over a fire in the side yard. Grams said I wasn't big enough to stir the whites, but I was "just right" to turn the crank on the wringer that squeezed rinse water from the socks. "Careful now," Grams warned, "Don't get your fingers caught. You'll end up flat as a sock."

In summer Daddy parked our green 1939 Ford sedan at the top of the hill and we walked down to the house. Those walks were always a time for discovery. We had to check to see if the spring was running, if there was any cane left in the molasses press, if the cherries were ripe yet. Were the blackberries ready that grew along the garden fence? And we had to see how Grams' garden was doing this year. And sometimes we had to find an alternate route altogether because spring run-off had washed out a section of the lane.

But we never visited after Thanksgiving and not even then if it had snowed during the week. When Daddy said we were going for Christmas, I didn't believe him. But then he said, "We're taking the Greyhound Bus this time. Papaw'll meet us in town with the wagon."

A winter visit was too unusual not to raise some questions even for a five-year-old. And taking the bus was unheard of. I'd heard talk of gas coupons so maybe that was why. I liked buses because they smelled funny. Best of all, I didn't get carsick on buses.

Maybe we were going for Christmas because my uncles, Dad's three brothers, were overseas in the Army, and Grams and Papaw were lonesome. I wanted to visit the farm, but I worried about not being home for Christmas. How would Santa Clause find me down on the farm?

Daddy reassured me, "Santa knows when you're bad or good. He'll know where you are." I caught Daddy giving Mamma a wink over my head.

The bus ride from Cincinnati to Mt. Vernon was four hours long and it snowed most of the way. I overheard Daddy wonder to Mamma if Papaw would be able to get into town to meet us. Brother cried and Mamma fed him a bottle and put him across her lap to change his diaper. Daddy recited "The Night before Christmas" for Sister and me. Daddy liked to show off his memory by reciting long poems he'd learned in school.

Papaw met us inside the terminal and helped Daddy carry our suitcases outside. At first I didn't see the wagon, but then I recognized Jenny and Bow,

Papaw's mules, but they were harnessed to a giant sled. "Papaw, where'd you get the sled?" I asked.

"I took the wheels off the wagon and put on the skids. . .Wheels don't work so good in snow." We piled into the wagon/sled, covered ourselves with quilts and set off for the four-mile trip home. Years later, I don't remember the wet or the cold, just the fun of riding in a mule-drawn sled.

Grams had dinner on the table when we arrived—boiled potatoes, bacon flavored green beans, pinto beans, and cornbread still warm from the oven. Homemade molasses and blackberry jam for dessert. To wash it all down, large glasses of milk from the root cellar, a short walk out the kitchen door. Grams had no electricity or running water in her home. No one seemed to miss it much, except in cold weather when nature called.

Grams' dinner table was a large slab affair big enough to seat all her nine children growing up, four girls and five boys. An oilcloth with blue flowers covered it. Looking down the length of the table I could see evidence of each child's leaving home by the amount of pattern still visible. The end where Grams and Papaw always sat was mostly white. My place by Papaw's right elbow was worn but still had tiny blue flowers visible; that was Uncle Joe's place–he was the baby. I missed Uncle Joe a lot, but was told, "He's serving Uncle Sam now somewhere in Europe."

After dinner, kerosene lamps were lighted and we all gathered around the fireplace in the mostly dark front room. All the rooms in Grams' house had newspaper glued on the walls which I thought was a grand idea because the pages by the bed where I slept had pictures on it from the Cincinnati zoo. The Ohio-bunch provided the newspapers, but Grams glued them on all by herself. Gram's only Christmas decoration was a few colorful cards on the mantel wedged in between framed pictures of my three uncles in their army uniforms. Grams took the cards down one at a time and Daddy read them aloud.

At five to the hour Grams moved one of the lamps over to a small corner table. In the center, perched on a crocheted doily, sat Papaw's most prized contraption. I always thought contraption was a funny name for a radio but that's what Papaw called it. Uncle Joe had bought it for them with his first army paycheck. Cables ran down to an automobile battery that sat under the table. Grams was about to turn it on when aunts and cousins began arriving. As they stomped the snow from their boots on the rug inside the front door, Grams hollered, "Shsss...it's almost time for the news." Chairs were brought from the dining room, and the grown-ups sat or stood in a semi-circle looking at the radio. The room filled with sounds of static as Grams turned knobs to find the station. To conserve the battery power the radio was used for only fifteen minutes each night. Its only purpose—to receive news from the front.

After the news, brightly wrapped presents appeared from nowhere. Mamma gave Grams the housedress we'd bought for her and Daddy gave her the sweet-plug he'd sneaked by Mamma's watchful eye. (Mamma didn't approve of women chewing tobacco.) Papaw got his customary new set of long-johns. Wrapping paper was collected and folded to be re-used, and if it was too crumpled it'd be ironed and used for shelf and drawer liners.

Suddenly in the midst of all the fun there came a loud knocking and jingling of bells at the front door. Someone sang out, "Ho, ho, ho."

Grams called, "Come-in." But the door didn't open. The grown-ups were looking from one to the other. I was scared. Tickly scared. No one spoke.

Papaw asked, "Who can that be? We're all here." He opened the door to a thin man in a red suit and white beard carrying a burlap bag. "Santa?" Papaw asked. "Where'd you come from?"

"The North Pole," Santa said and walked right past Papaw. Santa ho, hoed his way around the room and then opened his bag. I was excited, but Sis was scared and Brother started to cry. My cousins hid behind their parents' chairs until Santa pulled a package out and asked, "Is Billy here? Where's little Nancy?" He was gone as abruptly as he'd come. He said, "Can't leave my reindeer too long. They get restless." After he left, the room was quiet. Some of the grown-ups smiled, others looked confused and Grams cried.

Santa had given me an ironing board and a real electric iron. I was wishing Grams had electricity so I could heat up my iron when the front door opened again and everyone got all excited. There stood my Uncle Dan in his army uniform, all smiles. The cousins and I rushed him. We wanted to know if he'd passed Santa in the lane.

Kentucky Walk

MANY YEARS AGO, an old woman and a young child would take walks together around the farmlands. They would finish up the breakfast dishes, turn to look at each other and say, "Let's go for a walk."

With that, the day's schedule was set. It was always the same; the old woman hung her white apron—soiled slightly with splatters of bacon grease and a little damp due to hand drying—on a nail by the kitchen door. She adjusted her faded cotton dress over her angular frame, and her hands searched for strands of salt and pepper hair that may have escaped the twisted bun at the nap of her neck. All in order, she turned to the watching child and asked, "Are you ready?" And hand in hand the woman and child walked out the backdoor of the small farm house.

As always, the weather was warm, because these walks took place in the summer. Summer was the season this little girl came to visit the hilly farm of her favorite aunt and uncle. Unlike her home where she lived with her mommy and daddy, this house had no running water or electricity, and she never had to sit on the toilet alone. Auntie's outhouse was a two-holer.

The child ran slightly in front of the old woman pulling on her arm as they crossed the backyard under the choke-cherry tree which shaded the house from the morning sun. Letting go of the child's hand, the old woman lifted the wire loop off the pole which held the gate closed. The child could hear Uncle's voice scold, "Gotta keep that gate closed, Child. Can't have the cows coming into the yard. Why they eat everything in sight, and leave cow pies to be stepped in."

Woman and child followed the hard-packed, dirt path around and behind the barn. Barn smells stirred up memories for the little girl. The smell of dried tobacco never quite leaves a barn in Kentucky. In the fall, tobacco leaves are stripped from the stems and gathered into broom-sized bundles which hang on poles suspended between the rafters of the barn until they are dry and ready for market. That smell made the child's stomach feel sick. She remembered the time she and her cousin had tried to chew tobacco the way her grandmother did. She looked up at the tall unpainted barn and shivered with the memory of it.

Other smells were more pleasant, like those of corn and hay. The corn bins were almost empty this time of year and she could hear the rustling, scurrying sounds of mice hurrying around under the dried husks looking for the hard dried kernels which had been knocked loose from the cob. Auntie hated it when mice got into the house. She would take out after them with a broom, and the mice would run under the cupboard where the dishes and leftovers were kept. Auntie couldn't reach them there and they would be safe. The little girl hated it when the mice didn't run fast enough and Auntie hit them with her broom.

It would be time to mow the hay soon. Hay mowing was one of her favorite times. Uncle and Grandpa used huge curved cutting blades on a long rough handle to cut the hay. They walked slowly through the hay field swinging the scythe from side to side. She wasn't allowed to help on cutting days, only on hauling days. Sitting on the horses' backs and talking to them as they pulled the hay wagon was her job. Uncle and Grandpa walked beside the wagon and used pitchforks to load the hay onto the wagon. They could throw hay so high the wagon-load of hay would be as tall as the sweet apple tree before they headed back toward the barn. As an added bonus for helping with the horses, the little girl got to keep all the tortoises that Uncle and Grandpa found hiding in the hay field. She was always bringing home creatures she found out in the fields, much to the distress of Grandma, Auntie, and Momma.

The little girl let go of Auntie's strong, brown hand, and ran ahead. She knew exactly which way she wanted to go. Turning her face into the sun and following the deep ruts made by wagon wheels, she let the momentum of the slope carry her to the pond's edge. She was already wondering how many of yesterday's tadpoles had sprouted legs and crawled onto the slippery clay bank. Tadpoles, frogs, water bugs and pennywinkles could amuse her for hours. The pond was full of her wondering friends. She wondered how many tads had legs? How many still had tails? What happened to the tails? Did they fall off or get eaten? Where were the frogs' Mommys? Which ones are Daddys and which ones are Mommys? Where were the water bugs darting off to in such a hurry? Why didn't they sink?

What did they eat? Do they sleep in the water? What do the pennywinkles do when they grow bigger than their shell? Do they get tired carrying their house around all the time? Why are they so quiet? Wondering was one the little girl's favorite games to play.

Old woman and child squatted at the low edge of the pond, the side where Uncle leads the horses in to drink on his way from the fields to the barn. Side by side they paused, their chins resting on their knees. The child wiggled her toes into the damp clay bank. And for a moment, with the sun warm on their backs, the woman and child watched the black, fat-bellied tadpoles and marveled at the magic of life and change.

"Oh no! Auntie, we forgot the jar. How can we catch tadpoles without a jar?"

"We'll leave catching tadpoles for another day," Auntie said. "I have a different treat in store for us today. Come along. Let's go down through the back pasture to the woods."

Birds sang, bugs buzzed, frogs croaked, and woman and child resumed their walk retracing their steps, up the rutted trail to the path that ran along ridge. The child was careful to stay on the path and avoid the lacey white flowers that grew in patches of sun on either side of the path. She knew them as chigger flowers, not to be gathered or even touched because the result would be a spot bath with coal-oil. According to Grandma, chiggers don't like coal-oil.

As was the custom on these walks, the child darted ahead then returned to the old woman's side to show her some found treasure. Most often these treasures amounted to an acorn with hat still in place and would be christened the smallest ever or the biggest ever. Each was greeted with oohs and ahhs of admiration from Auntie, and the child would be off to find another worthy gift.

A call of "Look what I've found" would spin the child around and bring her running to Auntie's side. It might be the sighting of a discarded snake skin hanging high up in the branches of an ancient oak. Or Auntie would offer down a hand mounded with ripe blackberries or huckleberries. These handfuls came with the reminder, "Blow on the berries before you eat them. You never know when you might be sharing with a spider."

A tingle ran down the child's back as she stepped from the path into the woods, for she knew woods to be magical, and wondered what adventure she and Auntie would have today. Could it be that Auntie had found a new grapevine swing? She and Auntie had looked for the swing they used last summer, but it was nowhere to be found.

They passed through the woods and out the other side. This was a new place for the child, this bright sunny meadow filled with grasses and wildflowers. The goldenrod rose almost to Auntie's shoulders. There were daisies, dandelions, lavender, violets, and blue and purple flowers whose names she didn't know. The child ran into this lake of color with arms outstretched, causing the grasses and flowers to bow down as she passed. She ran in circles, and twirled until she was dizzy and fell to the ground laughing.

LEOTA MCGOWAN HOOVER died of breast cancer in 2014 before her memoir was published. She grew up in Arizona then moved to Alaska where she lived for twenty-four years. Due to her many adventures in that state, Alaska figures as a character in much  of her writing, as are moose, salmon and freezing weather. Her most transforming experiences came during her work with the renowned innovative thinker, Elizabeth Kübler Ross, who inspired her writing and shook her world. She received the 2008 first prize in the Professional Writers of Prescott's non-fiction contest and was a finalist in the *So to Speak* literary contest. Her personal essays have appeared in *2008 Byline Calendar*, *The Companion Parrot*, and *Threshold*.

Made in the USA
San Bernardino, CA
13 May 2020

71445462R00193